Trauma Has No Color

VOLUME TWO

TRADING THE MASK FOR A CROWN

SHARNETTE CARTER   TIERRA MOSLEY

AJA CHRISANTA   SHELLEY PUCHALSKY

ENERI   RENSKI

DEVARON FLINT   JORDAN QUANDER

DEBORAH JACKSON   VICTORIA ROSS

AUDREY LEE   DAPHNEY WALKER

ZIONNE MALLOY   B. WILLIAMS

PATRICIA WILLIAMS

LOGOS
COMMUNITY DEVELOPMENT
CORPORATION

ISBN: 979-8-218-10147-3

Published by Logos CDC

www.logoscdc.org

Harrington, Delaware

Printed in the United States of America

Contents

Forword

"Trauma Has No Color" was birthed out of the desire to see individuals shed the shame and confront the pain! Each year, courageous individuals come together and process their trauma in a therapeutic setting, creating an inspiring anthology.

The emotions are stored within the heart, and the heart reveals the photos of the past. Those photos produce memories that can cause you to crumble or to rise up! "Trauma Has No Color" reveals a recollection of memories of fifteen brave individuals that chose to flip through a portion of their photobook that caused them a tremendous amount of agony. These individuals did not submit to the pain; rather, they turned their pain into purpose and allowed it to propel them forward. The memories shared will challenge readers to flip through their own photobooks. These memories will also encourage and inspire readers to shed their shame, confront their pain, and start their journey toward healing.

-Dr. Teneshia T. Winder PhD, LMFT

CHAPTER ONE

The Weight Of Life

Audrey Lee

As a little girl growing up in church, I always heard the saying, "God doesn't put more on you than you can bear." But oftentimes, I wondered how heavy the weight had to be to not be able to bear it anymore. God has always been the center of my life, but that never stopped life from happening. As a young child, I struggled with grief, trauma, and suicidal thoughts, but my faith is what has held me together for 26 years.

About 16 years ago, the first weight was put on my shoulders. It felt as if someone had put one hundred-pound rock in a bag and asked me to carry them around the world. My best friend died. Kayla was her name. She had the sweetest voice, long silky black hair, beautiful chocolate skin, and a smile that could light up a room. The night I lost Kayla was such a gloomy and cold night. We were at our church with the rest of the youth, practicing for a youth conference that we attended every year.

We were all a part of a step team, and we would practice from sun up to sun down, perfecting our gift, but that particular night it was different.

When it was time for us to depart and go our separate ways, Kayla begged my mom to let me go with her. My mom repeatedly said no because a big snowstorm was coming, and she didn't like me being away from her for too long. I remember crying and begging my mom to let me spend the night with Kayla, but she wouldn't change her mind. My mom told my best friend that we would see each other on Sunday and to hug and say goodnight. That hug was different. That hug felt strange. I began to cry, and so did Kayla. Everyone kept telling us that we would see each other in a few days, but my gut told me differently. We all left the church and traveled to our own destinations.

I arrived home and went to bed, knowing I would be home the next day because of the snow and I could talk to Kayla on the phone. I woke up the next morning to my parents crying in the living room, and that's when they told me. Kayla Died. My world stopped. I couldn't process my feelings. I couldn't speak, my voice was gone, and my eyes filled with tears. All I could ask God was, why? God makes no mistakes right? At that moment, I felt like God had made the biggest mistake in the world. I remember Sunday came, and all the youth surrounded the altar for prayer, but I didn't want prayer; I wanted my best friend. I was mad at God, he took the one person I loved with all my heart, and she was never coming back. My mind was numb, my body was numb, and my heart was broken.

My pastor began to pray for all the kids, and we were all crying not out to God but out of pain. Finally, I dropped to my knees and screamed, but no sound came out. That's the moment the weight started to get heavy. I felt like I couldn't go on. I wanted to be with my best friend so desperately that I would do anything to make it happen. As months went by, I battled with not wanting to walk on this earth any longer, and one night I decided I had enough of living. I felt worthless, confused, hurt, and lost. Grief had its ugly hands around my neck to the point I felt lifeless. It was time for me to go. I didn't care about my family or friends; I just wanted the pain to stop.

I sat at my kitchen dining room table, thinking about how I wanted to die. I knew my mom had some pills that would accomplish my goal of not living anymore. I went through her medicine bag and found anything I thought would help remove the pain and set it on the table. I sat at the table with the pill bottles in front of me, deciding which one I would take first, but to my surprise, I wasn't alone in the house like I thought I was. My grandmother was home, and she came and asked me what I was doing. I told her I was ready to die and I was tired. My grandmother took all the pills away, grabbed my hands, and began praying.

My grandmother has always had a relationship with God but never outwardly. At that moment, her prayers for me made my whole world shake. My heart and my mind began to feel light, and with my grandmother's prayers, I knew it wasn't my time to go. My grandmother never shared this with anyone, and she held this piece of me until her last breath.

As time went on and life went on, I was still bearing the weight. They kept adding up, like adding vegetables to a weighted scale. I went through life like any typical teenager, but life was still hard. I never really felt like anything good would happen to me until I met HIM. He was the guy that made me feel like I was the only girl in the world and that his love and God's love through him would fix every broken piece of me. In 2018, he and I began dating. I loved everything about him, from his voice to the nice-smelling cologne he would wear. He became my world, and no one could tell me different.

In 2019, he asked me to be his wife in front of our family and friends, and once that journey to the altar fast-tracked. I was so excited to be his wife that I didn't focus on anything else that was happening, especially in the dark. We set a date of August 29th, 2020. That was my wedding day. The happiest day of my life, right? We said I DO, and began our journey as husband and wife, not knowing what was up ahead of us. First, comes marriage, then comes baby? Well, for me, not so much a lot of tears, a lot of negative pregnancy tests, and a lot of worrying. But that all changed three months into our marriage. I WAS PREGNANT.

We shared the news with our family and friends, but devastation hit, and we lost the baby. I cried and cried, not understanding why God took the very thing I was praying to him the most about but he wasn't as devastated as me. Our marriage kept progressing, but the affection was nowhere to be found. I felt like I was living with my roommate. I felt like I was invisible. I never said anything about my feelings. I went to God in prayer, but slowly the little girl I thought was fixed started returning again. Then tragedy struck our marriage. My grandmother passed away. I felt like the wind was punched out of my chest, watching the undertakers take her body away. I felt numb, but I had to be strong for my parents. Dealing with my grandmother's death and still trying to be the best wife I possibly could, I lost myself. I had no ambition, no dreams, and no goals.

Whatever my husband wanted to do with his career and dreams, I supported him the best way I knew how but I was depressed. Depression wrapped me up like a warm blanket on a cold night and never let me go. I couldn't do anything, but no one understood. All I wanted was for my husband to give me a hug or a shoulder to cry on and understand that I was broken. I felt like no one could fix me, but to my surprise, someone did fix me for a short time. Then, I found out I was pregnant again.

I felt like this pregnancy was just what I needed to help me find my purpose in life, but six weeks later, that baby was gone. I cried and pleaded with God to let there still be a heartbeat even though I saw my baby leave my body. I felt like my body hated me, God hated me, and my husband hated me because I couldn't give him the one thing he desired. My depression got worse. I still went on with life like everything was okay, but inside I was hurting. December 4th, 2021, the life I thought I was going to live for the rest of my life STOPPED.

My husband asked me for a divorce. The anger and rage that filled my body were indescribable. I felt like I was falling into a dark hole, and no one was there to catch me. The embarrassment and disbelief I felt when going through our separation and divorce was exactly how I felt the day I lost my best friend. Numb, lifeless, worthless. I wanted to disappear off the face of the earth, but I felt like I failed at the one thing I thought I would be great at: being a wife. I felt like I was left with nothing, but then I realized I had God, my therapist, family, and friends.

My life has been full of weight, but now I know that God truly doesn't put more on you than you can bear. I'm bearing every weight that has been designed for me with grace and love. I finally understand that every battle and tragedy I have experienced has graced me for my career and future. And I know that all things work together for God's good.

LETTER TO SELF

Dear Younger Self,

Our life has been full of weights but now I know that God truly doesn't put more on you than you can bear. We will go through some trials that we will feel like we can't go on with life but guess what we can make it. We will try and try to figure out who we are but eventually all the pieces will come together. We will bear every weight that has been designed for us with grace and love. You will finally understand that every battle and tragedy that we have experienced in our life has graced us for our career and future. Just like we've been taught that all things work together for God's good.

CHAPTER TWO

Love, New York Karen

Renski

Dear North Carolina Karen,

I am sure leaving New York in 1972 when you were 10 years old was traumatic for you. Everything changed. In New York, you were joyful, "king of the hill", accepted, had friends, extended family, you were good in school, you laughed hard, played hard and loved every second of every day.

In New York, your mother was involved in her own life. She seemed happy, belonged to country clubs, ate at the finest restaurants, and shopped at the finest stores. In New York, your mother ignored you, but that did not matter, because your happy life did not involve her.

In August of 1972, your life changed. Your joy ceased. Your father, mother, 3 sisters and beloved dog moved to North Carolina. You were told the news on August 27th and the next day the movers arrived. There was no time for "goodbyes".

Upon arriving at your new home, you were enrolled in the only private school in the area. An Episcopalian school, which you were told was the "best and only option". Your first year there was a horribly traumatic one for you. You failed the 4th grade, on Christmas Day, your beloved dog passed away, your grandfather died, your great-grandmother died, and your beautiful cousin committed suicide. In addition, you were no longer "king of the hill", you weren't accepted, you had no friends, no extended family, you failed in school, you didn't laugh, you didn't play, and you despised every second of every day. Your family was the only Jewish family in school. You were labeled, the "Jew". You began to feel different and strange and saw yourself as an eyesore and outsider. You were taller, larger, had dark curly hair and green eyes. You were different.

Within weeks of moving, your mother's behavior changed drastically. Out of her element and miserable, she convinced you to feel the same. She demanded that you resent your father and daily insisted that you tell him how you (she) felt. She became emotionally abusive which ranged from calling you "fat", "stupid", "an idiot", verbally shaming, humiliating, ridiculing, and embarrassing you in public. When you did speak, you were attacked, shut down, invalidated, and belittled. Your feelings were insignificant. Your opinions and thoughts silenced. Your emotions became intense, but with no voice, your emotions came out in the form of tears. You were told you were "too sensitive", "overly sensitive", "that's just Karen, she'll cry at anything". You began to feel stupid, never enough, and inferior. Once a LOUD and PROUD little girl from New York, you were quiet, scared, rejected, introverted, stifled, and emotionally abandoned. You began to hate your body, your mind, your tears. You became invisible.

You were embarrassed and ashamed. Your grades in school were F's and D's. Your confidence was hit even harder by being picked last for spelling bees and sports. Your parents threatened to send you to public school because you were a failure and stupid. To your parents, public school was where the poor, the inferior, and the "colored" went.

You were stifled and scared and afraid to talk because no matter what you said, it was wrong, stupid, and invalidated. Your mouth was permanently sealed shut, which was a way to protect yourself. Your mother hated silence. Whenever you were alone in the car with your mother, she began screaming at you. She looked at you angrily and yelled, "talk damnit, talk!". You froze. She began screaming louder, and said, "well if you are just going to sit there like a stupid idiot, then at least read the signs/billboards on the road, unless you are too fucking stupid to do that." Those car rides felt like an eternity. Trembling and frightened, you read every billboard, restaurant sign, and street name that passed.

The rejection and abandonment became debilitating. For your 11th birthday, you requested a vanilla cake with vanilla ice cream. Your mother laughed, shook her head, and said, "Ewe! Really? That's disgusting!!!". That night they presented you with "your" birthday cake, sung to you, and then disserted you. You were left to eat your birthday cake alone. You felt ridiculed and abandoned for asking for what you wanted.

In the kitchen, your mother had an "off-limits" cabinet. It overflowed with her favorite cookies, crackers, and candy. One day, you crept into the "off-limits" cabinet, opened a box of Oreos, and took three. You manipulated the Oreo-lined rows by taking one from each row in hopes that she would not notice. Within hours, your mother screamed, "WHO ATE MY OREO'S!!!". She ran to your bedroom, flew open the door and started screaming and pointing at you saying, "you ate my Oreos, now you are going to pay!". She ran downstairs, slammed open the garage door, got in her car, and screeched off. Within the hour, she had returned with a grocery bag filled with 10–15 boxes of Oreos. As she approached your bedroom, she was screaming violently. She swung the door open and demanded that you eat it all. You froze, started crying, and began shaking. You denied it. You pleaded with her to believe you. She snatched the up the bag and proceeded to pound on your sister's door. Your mother berated, belittled and fat shamed her as well. She demanded that your sister eat every Oreo in that bag. In the weeks following the Oreo incident, your parents bought a mirror and placed in front of your sister's plate. She was forced to watch herself eat and was not permitted to get up until she finished her meal. To you this was disturbing, cruel and inhumane. You felt horrible, shamed, scared, and frightened. You let it happen and didn't know what to do. For years you feel guilt and above all shame. You became bulimic, and that continued for 25 years. Ten years ago, you apologized to your sister for what you caused. Three years ago, you were no longer bulimic.

You were frightened of your mother's erratic behavior; it came out of nowhere. You didn't understand her intense anger. She became "angry scary mom" and "violent temper mom". Her silent treatments were debilitating. She would slam down phones while you were speaking, slam doors in your face, shout, yell, and scream. She would grab her car keys and squeal out of the garage. She would be gone for hours, never knowing when she would return.

Your parents paid for you to graduate high school and to get you into a private women's college in Maryland. You majored in art. Your mother said that this was the best degree for you seeing that you had "no book sense". When they dropped you off at college, you felt that you should have been sad and scared, instead, you felt liberated, relieved, and excited. You marched into your dorm and began making friends, passed your classes (some A's even). You were in your element and began to discover who you were. That spring your parents came up for parents' weekend. When they arrived, they were greeted by a loud, proud, happy, bright, ambitious, and successful daughter. They did not know who you were. They said that you had changed. It was true you had changed. They did not like that and brought you home in the middle of your sophomore year. You were accepted to North Carolina State Universities, School of Design. In art school, you began to continue to evolve and spent less and less time at home.

The last family vacation you took was in 1984 to Jamaica. You were 22 years old. You were becoming a creative and independent individual. Your hair was cut like Prince's (in Purple Rain), you began dressing very funky, your "voice" was creeping in. This was not received well. You were made to look a "certain" way, talk a "certain" way, dress a "certain" way, and present yourself a "certain" way. Individuality was not an option. The first night in Jamaica, you were walking from the bungalow to the restaurant. Your mother was walking in front of you. She turned around to inspect what you were wearing. You were wearing her favorite color, navy-blue. You had on navy-blue shoes, a navy-blue skirt, a navy-blue cardigan and under that cardigan, you had on a plain white T-shirt. She stopped in her tracks, asked you where you got that shirt, and without notice, her hand went back, and she slapped you so hard across your face. It stunned and shocked you. My father and sisters said nothing and did nothing to protect you. That was December 23, 1984. Your mother did not talk to you again until January 3, 1985. During the entire vacation she would not look at you, address you, or speak to you.

While on vacation in Jamaica, your beloved dog passed away on Christmas day. Your mother didn't talk to you and left you alone while everyone was able to grieve together. You felt isolated, abandoned, and disserted. That Christmas day, you became stoic, abrupt, aloof, numb and had emotionally checked out. You knew that that was the end of the end.

Two months after returning home from Jamaica, you bravely escaped. You were 22 years old. You packed a bag, had $50 and said, "fuck you". You wrote a letter, hired a taxi, and had the letter delivered to your family. In the letter you wrote, "I have fallen in love with a black man. Do not follow me. Do not look for me. I am happy." You knew that interracial relationships were not an option in your family. Your parents called black people "colored". Your father said, "the reason why there are different continents was to keep all races separate from one another".

You washed your hands clean; however, that was not the case for your family. They hired a private investigator to track you. Your mother showed up at your jobs and apartments, would look at you, cry, not say a word and leave. Two years later, they knocked on your apartment door and pleaded for you to contact your maternal grandmother. They said she was worried about and wanted to know what was going on. They had asked you if you would memorize a script to read to your grandmother. If you called her, they bribed you with an incredible offer. They said they would put me up in an apartment in DuPont Circle, Washington D.C., and send me to the Corcoran School of Art. I agreed. The script said, "You were sorry you did not contact her sooner. You were backpacking through Europe and attending art school in Paris". The script was a success. My parents were happy. My grandmother was happy. You were miserable, empty, and ashamed. You declined their offer to go to Washington and did not speak to them for two years.

One night, after work your sisters were waiting in the store's parking lot. They approached and said, "Mom's cancer had returned, stress causes cancer, you're the cause of her stress; therefore, you are responsible for killing her". You believed them. You shut down and blacked out mentally and emotionally for the next two years. You found out your mother died after reading her obituary. You called my father to extend your condolences. He said, "you are not welcome to the funeral, your mother does not want you there". You shut down again. You don't remember the next six months. You buried yourself in work at American Airlines. You went on autopilot, you worked 12-hour days, and blacked out.

What your mother believed about herself; you began to believe about yourself. You became her. You became angry, aggravated, annoyed, agitated, frustrated, petty and resentful. You became rigid and thought you were always right. You judged others and yourself. You criticized, rejected, expected, invalidated, verbally attacked, and criticized others. You ran away, you avoided and disassociated. You perseverated about others and assumed peoples' intentions were done in malice so you "killed them" out of your life. During your 30 years in therapy, you were put on a vast array of psychological medications. You were misdiagnosed with over 10 psychiatric disorders, from depression to anxiety, PTSD, C-PTSD, bipolar, ADHD, hypomania, social anxiety disorder, generalized anxiety disorder and manic depression. You were finally diagnosed with borderline personality disorder (BPD). BPD is a mental illness that severely impacts a person's ability to regulate their emotions. This loss of emotional control can increase impulsivity. It affects how a person feels about themselves, and how their behavior negatively impacts their relationships with others. You found Dialectical Behavioral Therapy (DBT). DBT is effective for people who have difficulty managing and regulating their emotions. It brings together mindfulness, distress tolerance, interpersonal effectiveness, and emotional regulation.

While in DBT therapy, you were able to reflect and recall a few special memories of your mother. She was a beautiful pianist and you loved listening to her play Beethoven's "Moonlight Sonata". Very rare instances of happiness occurred at home. You had a swimming pool, but she swam infrequently (she didn't want to get her hair wet). When she did get in the water, she became a different mother. She was happy, you were all happy. She smiled. She became vulnerable. She became a human. She became relaxed and loving. The pool, the water became a safe and happy place, a place where you were able to "be you" and to let your guard down.

Because of your trauma, you are the person you are today. You are a super organizer, efficient, a mover, a shaker, and a doer. You are accomplished! At 37 years old, you put yourself through college. You graduated with honors with a bachelor's degree in Psychology, and a master's degree in Special Education. You turned your trauma into something powerful. You now work with individuals with developmental and mental disabilities. Your goal is to help protect, nurture, believe and empower them. You are now a take charge woman. You achieve everything you set your mind to. You are solution driven and have become a success.

You may have never thought that the traumatic events that you endured in your life would ever become a gift, but they have. Your mother gave you the gift of organization, party planning and an appreciation for classical music. Your gift from college was that you were able to see who you were always meant to be, a creative, loud, proud, happy, bright, ambitious, and vibrant woman who loves every single minute of every single day. You received the gift of acceptance, loyalty, protection, trust, and validation from your close circle of friends. My beloved dogs gave me the greatest gift, that of unconditional love, peace, joy, comfort, belonging, affection, attention, and emotional support.

I am so very proud of who you have become today. You are accomplished, empathetic, motivated, giving, and caring. You speak out and will not tolerate human and animal cruelty, prejudice or hate. You have become a fierce warrior who has a voice and uses it. You are amazingly LOUD and PROUD,

Love,

New York Karen

CHAPTER THREE

Gambling Is So Anonymous

Jordan Quander

It was a summer like no other. I was about to graduate high school in the summer of 2005 by the grace of God. I hadn't been living with my family since I was 16. I was staying with my friend Jackie and her mom, paying to sleep on the sofa with my old trusty Chevy Cavalier. I was working two jobs to support myself, one at "Where pigs fly" as a waiter and another at the Sunglasses hut in the mall. I thought I was doing something. I saved up enough money to get my first car with payments that summer, a Fire Escape. No one couldn't tell me I wasn't fly. That SUV took me places in my life and sheltered me in more ways than one. That was also the summer I met and fell in love with Melvin. It was a day like any other day in my hectic life. I was rushing from one job to another when I saw a familiar face.

When I was younger, my mom worked for a TRIO program, Upward bound, during the summer months. My sister and I would help with a lot of the clerical work putting IDs together and stuffing new students' folders. I saw a familiar face Melvin in the mall. He was working at the subway in the mall. I would often go to Subway to look at him and flirt. He was tall, 6'2 ", with nice, clean white teeth and long hair that he kept braided. I would often think about him and if he was available to date. There were a few times when he asked for my number. After he kept asking, I finally gave in to him. After a few phone conversations, I found out he had a son that was not yet a year old and had been in two long-term relationships that ended badly. After some time, I found out that his fiancé had been dating my cousin while they were breaking up. Talk about an awkward situation! After a few months of dating, Melvin and I decided to become a couple.

After a few days of us making our relationship official, one of my friends from high school came out and said that I stole him from her cause they were talking at the time. After several conversations with both her and me on three-way, it came out that was not the case. That should have been the first red flag. But inexperienced me, I decided to continue dating him. We spent a lot of time together getting to know each other and hanging out. Because he lived in his trailer, but his mom and sister moved in after their relationship fell apart. There was no place in the trailer for us to have alone time, so we often rented hotel rooms and spent time out at the movies and eating out. We decided to attend prom together because it was my senior year in high school, and he would be graduating from Delaware State University.

After some time, Melvin and I decided to move into his best friend's apartment, where we could have a room to ourselves. During this time, Melvin and his best friend would go out and spend time at the Casino on Friday and Saturday nights. At the time, I was not bothered or threatened by these actions. I was working overnight at the weekends at Wawa on route 8 in Delaware. A few weeks later, Melvin had asked me to borrow $20, and I thought nothing of it. I just assumed he could not get to the bank to take money out for gas. Then later that night, he gave me $80. He then told me he had gambled away his whole paycheck the night before and went back that morning and put the $20 I gave him into the machine and got it all back. I told him to let's be thankful he was able to do that but let's not make it a habit. He then took the time to reassure me that it was a one-time thing and it wouldn't happen again.

A few weeks later, I started to notice that he was still in the same cycle of gambling and borrowing to try and win the money back. This started to become a trend for Melvin even when I switched jobs to only working at Lowes during the day. He would still go to the Casino at night and gamble his entire paycheck. At one point, he did not pay his friend who we were staying with the rent, and he then looked to me for the money. This caused me to start questioning what he was doing with his money. After asking Melvin several times where his paychecks were going, he said he was in the hole with the bank. I asked him how much he said a lot. A few weeks later, riding in his car, I saw notices from the bank saying he was overdrawn for $600.00. After that, with the combination of him doing all these things and putting where I sleep at risk, I decided to leave him and move back in with my parents.

He moved back into the trailer with his mom and sister. While broken up, he said he had seen the error in his ways and wanted to get back together. I had also switched jobs. I started working at Wachovia bank. Once we decided to get back together, I found out I was pregnant with my oldest son Alexander a few weeks later. Melvin was upset but wanted to move in together. So I asked him to find us an apartment or place to rent. He had applied to two places and was denied by both. He looked into getting another trailer in the development. Due to his bad credit, we were not able to be approved. Melvin never told me he was also behind in his car payment and credit cards due to his gambling. I decided to find a place for me and my new baby before I went into labor.

My mom helped me locate some income-based apartment complexes that would accept someone that was pregnant. I found one, "The Laurels." I was able to save up enough money despite the financial issues Melvin was having and him nickel and dimming me for money. When I moved into my apartment, I was so proud of myself. I was able to get a few things from the store cause my credit wasn't shot then. Melvin moved in with me to my new apartment with my contact stating he would make an effort to pay off his past due bills and pay at least $50 a week towards the rent. Melvin was upset about the arrangements but agreed to the terms. During this time, Melvin would often come home to the apartment and go out with his friends from work. They would often end up at the Casino. But I didn't say too much about it cause I was able to maintain the apartment with my own money. It wasn't until I started noticing that small amounts of cash in the house would go missing.

I began to make sure I didn't carry cash on me. Then another day, I noticed that my credit and debit cards were missing. I waited till Melvin got home and asked where my cards were. He then admitted he had been taking them and using them. My heart sank. Here I was, trying to make a place for me to raise our child, and he was doing everything in his power to make it so I couldn't afford it anymore. From that day forward, I got a safety deposit box at the bank and made sure I placed my entire wallet in it every night. My due date came, and I gave birth to our son. The day after I gave birth, Melvin forgot to pack a go bag. So he told my family and me that he would go home, shower, stop, get me some food, and return within a few hours. He left my bedside at 10 am and did not return till midnight without clothes. I was upset and automatically knew where he was. I maintained my composure and continued enjoying my new baby's birth. I forgave him and asked what I could do to help him with his debt. That year I got my taxes back and paid off his payday loans. I informed him that this was a one-time deal and I would not be able to do it again. But we all know it was a lie. I helped him again by putting another $600 into his checking account, hoping it would help him get back on track after a lot of back and forth over the year until Alex was about to turn 1.

I had a conversation with myself and decided that as much as I loved him, I could not allow him to stay in my life with my son and me financially. I told Melvin I could not afford him and loved him but could not let him bring me down. I told him I had goals and dreams that I would never be able to get to if I stayed in a relationship with him. So I dropped Melvin off at his co-worker's house and never opened that door again.

It was very traumatic for me to live in that situation with Melvin. I became an invert. I was outgoing when we first met, but I became a person that kept to myself. I often feared going home on pay days because I knew he would be there and ask for money. I started to develop a low tolerance for people asking me about my personal life and how my pregnancy was progressing. I remember being two weeks overdue trying to put together a crib while Melvin was in the other room sleeping off the money lost from the night before. I started to develop anxiety regarding my future and my sons. I began to try to find ways to save money to make sure we were never in the position of being evicted. I had dreams more like nightmares about my inability to pay the bills in my apartment, not having anywhere to go, and him not caring.

I remember one time I was in the store, getting groceries. I only had $40 to last for four people till my next payday. Melvin never helped with the bills even though he was working. I burst into tears and was so mad that I had to nurse my son to calm my nerves. I also had insecurities about my ability to learn. I did not tell a lot of people, but I had an IEP. I had never shared that with anybody. Melvin knew that and used to make fun of me for the issues I had with learning, but that was his way of making himself feel better.   As in love as I was with Melvin, I started to notice the changes that had become my normal cause of what he put me through.

I had so much trauma surrounding living with him while he was in addiction that it took me years to figure out all its effects on me. I am jaded when it comes to relationships. I do not trust easily; I question everything someone is telling me. I have anxiety when it comes to making sure my kids are taken care of. I often work myself to the bone to make sure my son does not go without. I snap at people when I get mad. I have discovered I have become a doom day, hoping for the best but preparing for the worst. Also, I shield my son from a lot of things. He did not even know his dad had issues until this past summer. When I hear a man say he goes to the Casino or plays the lottery, I do not even entertain him for another minute. I just keep pushing cause to me; he is not worth my time.

After I ended the relationship, I found the courage to move out of Delaware for a year to try and gain different employment. I started to have a social life with my group of mom friends. I returned to school and completed two Associates degrees in Human Services and another in Drug and Alcohol counseling. I am currently trying to complete my bachelor's in social work. That relationship showed me that I am a lover, and I love hard and want to see the best in people even when they are giving me the worst. I am family-oriented, and no matter what, I can heal from whatever I have gone through.

CHAPTER FOUR

I Did What I Thought
I Should Have Done

Sharnette Carter

I've always tried to do what I was supposed to do. I've always tried to do the right thing, be responsible, be pragmatic, and follow the rules. I knew what was expected of me and I've always tried to meet those expectations. My family, my fluctuating faith, community, and society set some expectations. I've lived in a problem-solving survival mode for most of my life. That's why I got married.

I have had no contact with my family. I hadn't spoken to anyone I was related to in almost a year. I wasn't interested in dating and had an extremely small circle of friends. I was working and going to school full time. I was planning to leave the country when I completed my degree to teach abroad for a while and was seriously considering joining the Peace Corps. I had goals and hopes for my future. I really enjoyed making plans and looking into different possibilities. I focused on what I wanted for my life and what would make me happy. For just a moment, the only expectations that mattered were my own. I was in this space when I met my ex-husband.

I was shopping in the springtime. He saw me at the door of the supermarket and greeted me with, "you look single". I was confused and continued walking toward my car. He followed me, which made me nervous, but he had a little boy with him. I figured someone had entrusted him with this small child so he couldn't be that bad. We stopped at my car and chatted for a moment. I gave him a phone number and waited until he was gone before I started my car and drove home. I remember recounting this event to a close friend. I was nervous. I wasn't sure if I had given him my actual phone number or the flipped fake number, as was my intention. We giggled, and I brushed it off. Turns out, I'd given him my actual number.

He called and we talked, and he seemed like a nice guy. Correction, he was a nice guy who was completely into me. He called me all the time and we talked for hours. Finally, we agreed to go out on a simple date, like dinner and a movie at the mall. I arrived first and watched him walk in. I had only seen him once before, when we first met and boy, reality didn't match the image I had made of him in my mind. I panicked. Was it too late to just leave? Would he see me? Oh god! He saw me and his face lit up. I had to be nice, right? It would have been so rude to cancel at that point. What excuse could I give him? "Uh, you look different than I had imagined." What sense would that make? I'd seen him before. Plus, that would have been incredibly rude and superficial. He was a nice guy.

I needed to be nice, I needed to uphold my end of the agreement. We got dinner at the food court, and I watched him slather his sandwich with mayo. Like an unreasonable amount of mayonnaise. It dripped from his sandwich and got all over his face with each bite. My heart sank; I was disgusted. I wanted to leave. I reminded myself of our great phone conversation. I reminded myself that personality was more important than looks and table manners. We went to see the movie. I got over myself, and I didn't have a bad time. He was sweet and drove me to my car at the end of the date. He was completely into me. He accepted me for who I was. I didn't have to prove my worth to him. I was good enough for him. I had NEVER felt that way before. I always had to hide bits and parts of myself or put on an act to feel accepted. I didn't have to do any of that around him.

Things moved WAY too fast after that. We went on a couple more dates. The little boy with him the night we met was his son. He and his son's mother had split up not long before we met, and he had moved out of the apartment they shared. He wasn't going to work at the time because he had recently had surgery on his knee, and he was living with his mother. So, he had plenty of time on his hands, and he spent much of it with me.

That summer, I found out I was pregnant. I was still in school, I was still working, I certainly wasn't ready for a baby. I considered my options, and he convinced me that he would be there and help take care of the baby. I would be able to finish school. He had returned to work at this point and immediately started looking for a second job. He moved into my tiny two-room apartment. He encouraged me to reunite with my family. At Christmas, we got engaged. He accompanied me to many of my prenatal appointments and attended my two baby showers. That winter, our daughter was born surrounded by family, friends, and many nursing students. My baby girl and her father watched me walk across the stage and receive my degree. That summer, we all moved into a house together. His son moved in with us also. It wasn't what I had planned for myself, but it was good, right? There were so many women who wanted what I had, a family, a ring; that's what I was supposed to want so I thought.

That fall, I found out that I was pregnant again. I was embarrassed. Who has back-to-back babies like that? How would we be able to afford it? I still haven't found a teaching position yet. We weren't even married. I had pushed the wedding back further and further because we didn't have the money. I had come to learn that I didn't really like family and wasn't excited about it. I didn't care. I just did what I was supposed to do. I was living with this man and was having another baby with him. That's not how I was raised. That's not how I was supposed to do things. Then, I feared the Church of Jesus Christ of Latter-Day Saints, the LDS. My ex-husband was LDS and was fathering his third child out of wedlock. I knew of a woman who had been excommunicated for having children out of wedlock. I didn't want that for my children's father, a man I cared about. I didn't agree with much of the LDS doctrine, but if that's how he found God, I didn't want him to lose his faith because I was hesitant. I heard the LDS home teachers asking him when he would get married. I looked up how to get a courthouse wedding, and we married in the spring.

I started my first teaching position in the following fall, one month after the birth of our son. It was challenging, as the first year of teaching always is. In addition, I had a brand-new baby, and I was teaching a course I was neither hired to nor certified to teach; not only that, my classroom was in a trailer that leaked and leaned. I brought in furniture from home and pieced together a learning environment. On top of that I was nursing and had to cut through another classroom to get into the main building just to go to the restroom. Through that, my ex supported me. He cared for the kids when I wasn't there, which was often. I wasn't unusual for me to stay at work until 10pm and sometimes get to work an hour early.

I was not rehired at the end of the school year. I was "riffed", Reduction in Force. I received positive evaluations and recommendations so I was able to find a new teaching position during the summer. The following school years, I noticed a change. I didn't feel like I had a partner anymore. I constantly corrected his mistakes like spending the bill money, giving things away, and being rude to service people. It was exhausting. I had to tell him what to do all of the time. It was like I had another kid in the house. I had to tell him and the kids to clean up after themselves all of the time. All he would do was play Madden on the Xbox. I felt abandoned. I was tired all of the time and was no longer attracted to him. I told him it was like I had brought one of my students home. I was parenting him as well as the children. I stayed late at work all of the time. Very late, like until six or seven pm. On days when I didn't have much work to keep me after school, I would sit at the park and read for hours before going home. Later, when we moved and the park was no longer a convenient location, I would go home. At this point he was going to the gym daily and taking the kids with him. I would pretend I was asleep when he got home to avoid talking to him.

I had given up on the marriage. I was looking forward to the day when the kids were older so I could leave him. I literally wanted to die. Dreams about dying weren't nightmares to me. Often, I would wake up disappointed that I had woken up at. I had stopped doing house chores. No one did anything in the house. I was cleaning up after all of them. I was exhausted. I didn't know what to do. I wanted to stay so the kids could have a two-parent household. I didn't want to be a black single mother stereotype. I felt trapped and like the only way out was the grave. I stopped taking my diabetes medication and ate whatever I wanted. I didn't care anymore. I was miserable.

My husband was also unhappy. He started leaving out after he dropped of the kids from the gym. I didn't care. I was glad that he wasn't in the house. Then he took a week off and started staying out all night, coming home just in time to be with the kids while I went to work. At first, I didn't care until one morning; he didn't come home at all. Before heading to work, I had to rush to prepare the kids for school and take them to their grandmother's house. I was livid. How could he be so inconsiderate? I didn't care where he was, just that he was disrupting the logistics of the day.

Eventually, I became tired of this dynamic and told him he needed to move out of my house. He didn't argue or try to convince me to let him stay. That was when I began to think he was cheating on me if he had a place to stay. Eventually, it came out that he had been seeing someone. I was more insulted than hurt when I pulled up her Facebook profile and saw who she was. I didn't understand then why he was with someone like her. Her posts indicated that she liked drama and attention. At the risk of sounding snobby, she came off like trash. She was a downgrade. It was a hit to my self-esteem because she wasn't conventionally attractive. Is that the kind of woman he wanted? Was I the same caliber as her? Was I ugly? Did he think I was trashy? I felt like I wasn't good enough, but what he liked, what was good enough for him, was garbage. Was that garbage better than me?

I had made those assumptions based on what I'd seen on social media. After years of dealing with her and her family, I proved that my assumptions were correct. She was trash, and she loved drama. He moved in with her the day I told him to leave. They were engaged to be married a month later. She accompanied him whenever he came to get the kids and made her presence known. She would shout from the car that she was in front of my house. She came to my job to cause trouble and the school resource officer had to confront her. She authored emails to the school's principal, and even had a meeting with her where she accused me of harassing her and my husband during school hours. Fortunately, the principal knew me well enough to know that I wouldn't do anything like that. She had been in a similar tumultuous situation before, and I had her support.

I've had to make forty-three trips to family court in five years. Every court document filed was in her handwriting. She even petitioned for my divorce, and my husband signed it. They got married two weeks after the divorce was finalized. They had filed multiple rules to show cause that were dismissed, Protection from Abuse orders that were dismissed, and made several petitions to modify custody and visitation. Her mother followed me to a friend's house after a school event for the kids. The police had to get involved several times. They doxed me and told lies about me on social media. She threatened me several times.

I was in a constant state of alert. My soul left my body whenever someone would unexpectedly ring my doorbell. I was afraid to check the mail. I was so fearful that there would be more court documents, hearings, and accusations. My ex-husband and his wife made it their business to try to make me unhappy. They even came and stole the grill off the back deck because the kids mentioned I was planning a cookout for my family. I was so angry because I wanted to confront them, fight them, clap back, but I had to be the bigger person. I couldn't risk getting in trouble or giving them anything they could report in court documents. They were giving me enough trouble with their lies. I was also perplexed. I couldn't understand why they wanted to hurt me so bad. She had gotten the man, and he made sure I knew that he was with the love of his life. So why not leave me alone? What had I done to bother either of them? I didn't say anything to them. I didn't post about them on social media. I never stopped my ex from seeing the kids, even before a court order was in place. What were they getting out of all the chaos they were creating?

In 2019, tension started to form between my daughter and me. She became very resistant, argumentative, and subversive. She tried to come between her father and me, to try to protect him from the consequences of his actions. She often stood up for him and commented that I was being unreasonable when he violated the court order. I am sure that her father and stepmother were telling her that I was the cause of the drama and antimony between the three of us. She became part of their team, plotting and scheming so that she could go live with them.

It was becoming increasingly difficult to live with her. She started lying and stealing from me. She is the reason that I stopped carrying cash. She wrote letters to the courts saying she would rather live with her father because I was mean, and she had more fun with them. I told her that it was none of their business what happened in our home. I explained how they would take normal events and twist them in court documents. Child protective services were often at my house. I was accused of not feeding the children, locking them in the basement, and slamming her head against appliances. That last incident resulted in a Protection from Abuse order while it was investigated. The accusations were unsubstantiated by medical records, and the social worker reported all the inconsistencies in my daughter's story. She was released back into my custody.

A month later, one morning before everyone had to leave for their various schools; I saw that the kids had left the living room a wreck the night before. I confronted my daughter about it, and she became agitated, claiming she had nothing to do with the mess. She screamed at me, and I grabbed her arm and screamed back. I told her I didn't have time to argue and expected the two of them to clean the mess when they got home. That afternoon, the social worker came to close out the "dryer door case" and interviewed both kids. My daughter never mentioned the incident from the morning. The social worker closed the case and left.

The following day, the kids went with their father after school. They were very late getting back without explanation or apology as usual. My daughter gave some excuse as to why they were late, but days later, my son admitted that the story was a lie and that they had gone to the hospital and talked to the police. The following day was Friday, the weekend they were to spend with their father. I was out shopping for clothes for the kids when the social worker called to speak to the kids. She told me that there had been another allegation of abuse but because the police were involved, she couldn't give me more details. I put all of the clothes back and went home.

That Sunday evening, only my son came home. When I asked where his sister was, he simply replied, "they took her", and went on his way. A few days later, I got a phone call from a police officer asking about the incident. The following day, I got called to the principal's office because my ex-husband had emailed her about the PFA order and the abuse allegations.

The social worker and I talked about the number of reports being made against me and how risky it was to keep my daughter in the house. Other people said the same thing. I could lose my teaching license and livelihood because of those allegations. Anytime my daughter didn't get her way, she could run and tell her father that I had hit her or starved her, and he and his wife would jump at the chance to accuse me of abuse. My brother said, "that's a lot of power for a twelve-year-old." Many people who were aware of the situation said it might be good for my daughter to see what life was like with her father. I agreed with them, but I couldn't stop fighting for her.

I sat in the waiting room terrified. Where was the social worker? I hate that the only clocks in family court only seem to be in the courtroom. There was a heavy emptiness in my stomach and my heart fluttered all over my chest. Then, finally, the officer called me into the courtroom, and I went in alone. I always had to go in alone. Family law is so expensive; there was no way I could afford a lawyer. So I had to represent myself. I knew that I was telling the truth and that I was more logical and organized; I was smarter than them. But they had numbers. I knew they sat together, getting their story straight, making sure they all told the same lie. They would have learned that from the last hearing.

One at a time, they came into the courtroom and told their lies. I had to pay attention and stay focused. I had to contain my outrage and my pain. I stared at my ex-husband's wife as she sat on the stand and told stories of my daughter's distress, trips to the hospital, crisis centers, and police. I felt myself filling with anger and hatred. I stared at her: her antiquated tongue piercing, her cheap, gnarled wig, her outfit that looked more appropriate for a bar instead of the courtroom. I don't know if I hid my disgust well. I imagined how she smelled. I imagined a stench so pungent I could see it, a cloud surrounding her, like in the cartoons. She was filth in human form. I knew she was the mastermind behind all the lies being told. She was the catalyst. I wanted to attack her. I wanted to call out her lies, expose her, confront her, knock that crooked front tooth clean out of her mouth. But I sat there, silent, focused, listening, thinking of ways to poke holes in her story.

My daughter didn't look at me while she was at the courthouse. She glanced in my direction as she entered the courtroom but never made eye contact. That realization offered me a bit of vindication. She knew what she was doing would hurt me. I'm sure she felt it and now struggled to face it. I'd often wondered what I had done so wrong that she would go to such lengths to live with her father. What were they offering her? What were they telling her about me? What did she actually think of me?

She was dressed strangely. Not inappropriate or outrageously, just not like herself. The outfit was cute, but it wasn't "her". It wasn't something that she would ever pick out for herself to wear. I later saw that she was wearing the same thing her stepsister was wearing, just in a different color. She was on their team. It was a visual representation of the betrayal. Their way of showing me that she was one of them, that she had chosen them. I felt very alone. I felt like I had already lost.

I listened to her story and fought to hide my incredulity. I couldn't believe the lies! I was sure that the judge would see through the inconsistencies in all of their stories and would dismiss the allegations. He listened to everyone. Then he pulled out a big book and started listing this legal code and that legal code. He summarized. There was an event, and my daughter had an injury. Her injury was a split lip. Her lip had split because she never wanted to moisturize her skin. I wanted to protest. Where were the reports from the police and social worker? Didn't he know that correlation was not causation? None of that mattered. Based on the rules and the testimony, a reasonable person would conclude that the incident had caused the injury.

We left the courtroom. I was numb. I couldn't feel anything. I didn't have time to; I had to plan my next steps. I needed a hearing with my witnesses. I hustled to the self-service room and asked for the forms. I filled them out and submitted them immediately. I called the social worker several times over the next few days and told her what had happened. I wanted to scream at her. "Why weren't you there? You knew what was at stake and you weren't there?!" Instead, I asked that she would be present for the next hearing. I gathered subpoena forms. I didn't know what I was doing! I couldn't get legal aid because the allegations had been against me- I wasn't the victim. I felt hopeless, helpless, and exhausted, but I couldn't stop. I had to keep fighting.

A new hearing was granted a couple of weeks later. The social worker was with me. It was a waste of time. The judge said that I had filed the wrong form even though it was the form he had told me to fill out at the previous hearing. He told me to file a different form and sent us away. I had to swallow my rage. I didn't know what I was doing! I ran around in circles filling out the wrong paperwork while deadlines expired. Finally, I got a letter saying that my appeal had been denied. I lost my daughter. I never felt so defeated. I did what I was told to do. I was armed with the truth, but I still lost. I was sick. I was tired of fighting. I was tired of trying to be the bigger person, to be reasonable. I had run out of steps. There was nothing left for me to do but nothing.

Many people in my circle said that even though it hurt, this might be for the best. They said that maybe it was time for my daughter to see who her dad and stepmom really were and to see the truth finally. They said it was risky having her in the house when she didn't want to be there because she and her father and stepmother were going to keep causing drama and telling lies until they got what they wanted. I had to think about my son and my career- my livelihood. All of that was at risk while she was there, while her father and stepmom were plotting against me. It hurt to hear those things because I knew it was the truth. I had to let her go to have some peace.

I still don't know nor understand why my daughter went along with these plans. I've never talked about it with her, and I don't think I ever will. I don't want to hear that maybe I wasn't good enough for her. I don't want to hear how she was being manipulated and lied to. I don't think I could remain rational if I heard that she was okay with being used as a catspaw in her father's and stepmother's schemes. I had figured out what her father and stepmother wanted. They wanted to hurt me, and they wanted to see me fail. They tried to take my car, tried to humiliate me on social media and at public events. They tried to make me lose my job and teaching license. They wanted to take as much from me as possible because "losing" my husband wasn't a big enough loss for me. Yet, they saw my glow up, and that I had the support of friends and family. They saw that I was dating and enjoying myself despite their tricks. Taking my daughter was their trump card, the big joker, their final play.

They didn't realize that even though they had taken someone very precious away from me, they still left me with so much. I still had all the other things they tried to take from me. I still had my son. I still had my family, friends, car, house, job, and tomatoes on the back deck. The grass was still getting cut, and the bills were still being paid on time. My pantry and refrigerator stayed full, and we still had central air and hot running water. And in their plans, they had given me something I hadn't had in years. They gave me the peace of their absence.

They stopped coming to see my son. There were no more text messages, phone calls, or Facebook posts. All the drama just stopped. It felt like the calm after a nasty thunderstorm. There was minor cosmetic damage to the house, and the patio furniture had blown away, but there was calm. All I had to do was clean up. I felt guilty about enjoying this peace. They took my daughter! I should be distraught, in agony. I was sad, but mostly I was just tired. I was tired of going to court, I was tired of fighting these two unhinged adults. I was tired of having to be the bigger person. I was tired of fighting someone who obviously wanted to be somewhere else. I was happy for the rest, and that made me feel like I was a bad mother.

I also felt a little lonely. Halloween came, and I only had to make one costume. I only had my son with me to go to holiday events. We went to the local orchard and had a good time roasting marshmallow, sampling cider, and enjoying the hay ride we had been on so many times before. As we hopped off the hay trailer, we saw my daughter and the rest of her new family. She turned her head and made a very pointed effort not to look at us. Her stepsister greeted us awkwardly but politely. I returned her greeting. Her father tried to focus his attention on her, which seemed like an apparent attempt to ignore our son and me. Then there was her stepmom. She looked me dead in the face with a smug grin. I felt the bile rise in my stomach. I wanted to snatch that cheap, gnarled wig off her head and stomp it into the dirt. I wanted to slap the skin off her face and read her publicly for the filth that she is. Instead, all I could do was leave. I had to leave the orchard itself to avoid violating the PFA. I was seething internally. I'm not a criminal. I should be allowed to be in any public space I want, but I couldn't because of their lies.

My son and I carried on. He joined a club at school, but he was beginning to struggle. He was upset because they had taken his sister away. I could tell he was lonely, and I tried my best to support him. We traveled. Right before the pandemic, we spent a weekend in a cabin with friends in the mountains of West Virginia. The whole time, I kept thinking about how much my daughter would have enjoyed the trip. My son and I had a fabulous time, but I missed sharing that experience with her. Later, during the summer, my son and I went to Niagara Falls for his birthday. It was a great time: we sang songs in the car; we ate heartily and met many friendly people. Again, I often wondered how much my daughter would have enjoyed that trip.

I felt guilty about having such a good time without my daughter. But I knew I had to keep living; I couldn't just sit and be sad and pine away for her. It wouldn't be good for my son or me. People commented on how much happier I seemed and how I looked like I was at peace. I was at peace. There was no more drama. I heard absolutely nothing from my ex-husband, or his wife. They had gotten what they wanted and decided to leave me alone.

At the end of the summer, there was a court hearing to determine more permanent placement for the children. It was virtual, through Zoom, because we were still solidly in the pandemic. The judge awarded placement of my son with me and placement of my daughter with her father. Her ruling was ten pages long, detailing our testimony. The judge commented that my daughter seemed very indifferent when she spoke about me, and the judge inferred that it was a coping mechanism. The judge ruled that it would have been better for my daughter to have placement with me. Still, because we hadn't spoken to each other in months, it may not be mentally beneficial for the family. As a result, the judge modified the PFA so I could have overnight visitation with my daughter every other weekend. I was happy and nervous. I didn't know how my daughter would feel about me. Would she still fit in? Would she be comfortable? How would her father and stepmother behave when I showed up at their house for visitation?

The first weekend I was supposed to get my daughter was a failure. I showed up to the house with my son. Their car wasn't in the driveway. I called and texted her father several times. There was no response. We sat in front of the house for about a half hour and then we left. I was furious. They had the same court order that I had. They knew I was supposed to see my daughter that weekend. They just wanted to do whatever they could to keep her away from me. I felt let down. There was no way to enforce the court order. Even if I filled out paperwork, it would be months before any action. My ex-husband and his wife continued to violate the court order with impunity. All I could do was document the violation and move on.

On the following visitation weekend, my sister came along for the pickup. We parked on the road next to the house. The whole family was outside waiting for us. My daughter's stepmom approached the car for no reason. I noticed that she had a gun on her hip. She had her hand on it. I don't know what she was trying to say because I was so focused on the weapon. I told my sister to roll her window up. My ex-husband and his stepdaughter made a vast show of hugging my daughter and telling her goodbye like they wouldn't see her again. Finally, the stepmother moved away from the car, and my daughter hopped in the back seat. She smelled like a litter box! My son didn't care. He was smiling with his whole, entire head! He was so happy to see her. I was too horrified by the situation to feel anything. I just had to get away from the house. I sped off. The cat smell filled the car, and I noticed my sister roll her window down again. I asked her if she had seen the gun. My daughter told us that her stepmother wanted to ensure she had it on her when I showed up at the house.

On the way home, we stopped at Walmart to get her some things to wear over the weekend. She had obviously outgrown everything she had left at home. Finally, after almost a whole year, I was able to hug my daughter again! She was almost as tall as me. I could smell cat in her hair. I was so upset. Why was she walking around smelling like an animal shelter? What was really going on in that house? My sister and I bought her a few staples, and we headed home. We had breakfast on my mom's patio the following day, where my daughter told us "funny" stories about living with her dad. She regaled us with stories of animal feces on the floor, the absence of running water, and a dog urinating on her stepmother's wig and her stepmother still using it! We chuckled nervously at her stories, but we were stunned and horrified by what she told us.

At the end of the weekend, it was time to take my daughter back to her father's house. Since it was a long weekend, my daughter asked if she could stay an extra day. She asked her father before she asked me. He said that it was my choice. Considering our history and the fact that the PFA was still active, I decided it was best to follow the court order. I ended up taking her back to her father's house. My daughter understood. As we were on the highway, my daughter got a notification on her phone. Her stepmother had tagged her in a Facebook post. It questioned my love for my daughter as I hadn't seen her for months and declined extra visitation time. My daughter was visibly upset. "Why would she say this?" she asked. I wondered the same thing. Why was this woman so hellbent on trying to make me look bad to my daughter and her friends? Why would she post something so private and personal on the internet? She's a psychopath. I wanted to hurt that woman because she was always trying to provoke a confrontation. When we pulled up, they were all outside waiting. Her stepmother was there with her gun again. They made a massive show of greeting my daughter as though she had been gone for weeks. I both dreaded and looked forward to picking her up again.

The subsequent few visitations were the same. I was greeted by my ex-husband's family outside, and his wife's gun was visible during pickups and drop-offs. They always made a show of greeting my daughter and seeing her off at every visitation. I hated going to their house. I missed the days of the safe drop-off point at the state troopers. One time when I dropped my daughter off, her stepmother ran after my car shouting. Pickups and drop-offs were extremely stressful. During this period, my ex-husband resumed visitation with our son. Our son wasn't allowed at his house, so his father would pick him up and just drop him off at his grandmother's house for the weekend. Sometimes his sister would go with him.

During visits, more and more information about how things were at her father's house surfaced. She smelled terrible whenever I picked her up. She told me that she only had a good shower when she came to see me. She told me how her stepmother tried to coerce her by strangling her cat. She told me there was no working stove in the house, and the mice ran freely. I was appalled. I didn't know what to do, but I wrote down everything she told me.

On Veteran's Day, I visited a friend when my daughter called her brother through an app and said she was being kicked out of the house. I bolted home, picked up my son, and called the police while in route. Because there was still an active PFA, I couldn't be at the house outside of designated pickup and drop-off days. I also never went to her father's house without a police escort if it was outside the court order guidelines. When I got to the house, the police weren't there. I called to ask what had happened. They told me that the incident had been resolved and that the crisis center had been called. They wouldn't give me any other information, and I wasn't allowed to contact my daughter or her father to ask.

The next day, a friend asked if I was getting my daughter that day. Then she sent me a bunch of screenshots from Facebook. My daughter was arguing online with her father's mother-in-law. This grown woman called my daughter, a twelve-year-old, a tramp among other things on social media. No one corrected this woman. She went on and on about how my daughter was a liar, mentally ill and that her mother didn't love her. On the internet. I received these same screenshots again and again from several people. I needed to act. I asked several people to write letters detailing the interactions they had observed between my daughter and me. They reported how my daughter had told them they wanted to come home and what they had seen on Facebook. I printed out these letters and the screenshots. I was going to file for emergency custody- enough was enough. My daughter was not safe in her father's care. I was going to get my daughter's rendition of what was happening on Facebook and add that to the other documentation I'd been collecting.

Before I could even get to the courthouse to get the correct forms, her father texted to inform me our daughter was in an in-patient behavioral health facility. He informed me I wouldn't be able to see her. I felt my mind begin to spiral. My heart was racing, and I went into a panic. How would I find out what happened to my daughter? I sent a barrage of text messages and even risked calling. I received no other information from him despite my repeated requests. I knew that whatever had happened had something to do with the social media drama. Armed with this new development, I filed for emergency custody.

My daughter was in the facility for a week. While she was there, I was granted emergency custody. Still, I could not get any information about my daughter because her father refused to communicate with me. Eventually, I got a call from a concerned social worker. They had determined that based on what my daughter had told them, she would not be safe if she returned to her father's house. We started the process of bringing her home.

When I arrived at the facility a couple of days later, one of the workers pulled me to the side and told me that her stepmother was threatening to call the police because my daughter would not give her the clothes she was wearing. This woman literally involved the police in taking the clothes off the child's back! I wasn't surprised. I didn't even feel worried. As we left, her stepmother texted me not to go because the police were on the way. They'd have to catch me then. We drove off. I stopped at Walmart to buy my daughter some new clothes, and she changed in the bathroom. I called for a police escort so we could return the clothes and pick up my daughter's cat. When we arrived, no one was home. We dropped the clothes off and left.

I was a little nervous on the way home, but I was so happy. My daughter was coming back where she belonged. It took a while, but I was finally keeping her safe. When I entered our neighborhood, I saw her stepmother's big white truck parked near my house. I made a U-turn and went to a local pharmacy to wait for them to leave. I felt scared but ready to fight. It was the final showdown. Her father texted me repeatedly about the clothes and called. I ignored them until I was calm enough to respond rationally. He asked about his weekend visitation. I told him no and he could take it to court if he wanted to. I waited a few minutes and tried to go home.

When we entered the neighborhood, they were still there waiting. I parked a few doors down to call the police. Their stepmother pulled up behind me and blocked me in. I was terrified and incensed. I had to stay calm in front of the kids. Now wasn't the time to blow up or make an even bigger scene. Plus, I knew she liked to carry a gun around. She had to let me out of the space because she was blocking other cars. I parked in front of my house. My son was visibly upset. We got out of the car and started towards the house. The kids made it inside while their father yelled, "let's stop this madness!" The police finally arrived and got everyone's story. The evil stepmother wanted my daughter's school-issued laptop. It wasn't even signed out in her name! My daughter became frustrated with the situation and yelled at the adults from the front door. She had had enough. I didn't stop her. I knew that she had to let it out. I let her speak and then called her back into the house. I gave the police the laptop, and everyone left. Their stepmother squealed out of the parking lot shouting obscenities from the car. That was the last time I ever saw her. Good riddance, bitch!

I felt triumphant. I felt like I had beat the final boss of a horrifying video game I had been playing for years. Now came the work of helping my daughter settle in at home. Her father and stepmother still tried to give me trouble. I had to go to a few more court hearings and deal with a little more drama, but it was light work. Finally, I was awarded full placement of both my children; their father was not allowed to take them to his house. He agreed to the arrangement without any trouble. Not long after, their father and stepmother broke up, and she put him out of the house. He had to live in a shelter for a year. That's what you get! He had been humbled, and that monster he had married was out of my life for good.

My ex-husband still violates the court order and tries to be nasty to me when I don't bend the guidelines of the order to suit him. It's annoying. I'm still scared of checking the mail, and if some rings my doorbell, I feel like I'm going to faint. I still have a lot of healing to do. I'm always scared he is plotting some way to take the kids from me again and try to make me unhappy. I'm embarrassed that I allowed someone like him into my life, but I'm learning that he had a purpose, and I'm learning to accept that purpose. I don't trust him and don't think I ever will. I want my children to love him because he is their father, but I think I'll resent him for the rest of my life. I'll resent him for being weak and incompetent, for letting that woman mistreat my children and drag me through hell.

In this healing process for both my kids and me, I began to see them as individuals. They're great kids! We made it through it all together. I find these bursts of joy when I listen to them play video games, when they crack jokes at each other and at me. I worry about them, but I know they'll be okay. I understand that I'm only obligated to my children and myself. I'm learning to do what I want; not always what people expect of me. I haven't quite worked up the courage to say "No," but at least I find a way to avoid doing things I don't want to do. Small steps. One day at a time. I have to live my life for myself and be the best version of myself as an example for my kids. I enjoy myself as myself, for myself.

LETTER TO SELF

Hey,

How's it going? Not great? Yeah, sometimes it's gonna be like that. Sometimes the struggle is just too real, but you're gonna be okay. It's not rough all of the time. You can get through the rough patches, and then I need you to pay attention and enjoy when things are going okay. But it's okay that you're not okay right now. Just because you don't have it as bad as other people doesn't mean you're not allowed to be upset about how things are for you now. Your feelings are your feelings, and you can go ahead and feel them. Life is not fair, but it's okay; it's right; it's HUMAN to be mad when you feel like you're being treated unfairly. Be mad. Don't tear stuff up or hurt anybody but go ahead and be mad.

It's okay to be hurt. It doesn't matter if they didn't mean it or were "doing the best they can." If they hurt you, they hurt you. Remember, your mom says, "The road to hell is paved in good intentions." That applies to you, too. Be understanding, but don't let things slide cuz they didn't mean it. Let them know.

You don't owe anybody anything. You need to handle your responsibilities, but you're not responsible for everyone. You're responsible to yourself, for yourself. It's not being selfish so don't feel bad about not being able to help other people. You need to help yourself first.

It's okay. Your feelings are valid. It's okay to feel how you feel. No one can tell you how you should or should not feel. Even you can't tell you how you should feel. You should feel how you feel. It's okay. You're not overreacting or underreacting. Your feelings are right. Your feelings are okay.

Remember that. And it's okay to have boundaries. It doesn't mean you're being mean. You gotta protect you. If they don't like your boundaries, that's okay. If they don't like you, that's okay too. That's not a "you" problem. That's their problem.

CHAPTER FIVE

THAT GIRL

Tierra Mosley

So I wanted to give you some background on how I became "That Girl" because I wasn't always that way. Things happened in my life that pretty much forced me into places I never thought were fruitful. I'll get into all that later, but this is my story. I was born on September 7th, 1997. I lived with my mother, older brother, and older sister. Yes, I was the baby of the bunch. I don't remember much from infancy to my toddler years, but I do know that when I was about ten months old, my mother started dating my soon to be one day stepfather. We didn't have much coming up, but my mother made do with what she did have. We lived in an apartment for a few years. I was about 4-5 years old before moving to another apartment in a nearby surrounding city.

Let's fast this story for just a few years. In October. 2004 we moved into our first home. My mother's boyfriend, AKA my soon-to-be stepfather, bought us the house. Here is where I spent the majority of my known childhood and where the setting of the beginning of my story will take place. So we moved, my mother, married a year later, and many things started changing. She worked more, and we saw her less. At one point in time, I was always with her, up underneath her, and even slept in the bed with her from time to time. I was the baby of the bunch; I could do that, lol. I can honestly say that she was my first best friend. Until she wasn't.

My mother became so consumed with the life she wanted to present to people that she missed out on important parts of the little ones she created. She became so mean and so bitter. I remember coming home from school and literally dreading having to see her. She yelled, cursed, and screamed at my siblings and me a lot. My once okay/happy home became a not-so-happy home after a while. I did not realize what she was battling internally when I was a kid. How was I supposed to know that mom had been mentally, verbally, and physically abused, not to mention cheated on for years. Don't get me wrong, as I got older, I understood that my mom wasn't all so innocent, but I also realized that she wasn't fully to blame either. My mother's side of the family has dealt with a long line of mental illness, depression, and suicide.

As we all know, therapy wasn't a thing in black families, especially not ones in the church world. Many things were covered up and walked over as if they never took place. Which caused generational curses to hover over for decades ruling and roaming freely as if it was okay. I don't know much about what my mother endured as a child, but I am fully aware that she was sheltered and forced into keeping quiet about the things she saw and experienced. I'm not making excuses for her actions, behavior, or lack thereof because I'm a firm believer that once you get old enough to make your own decisions, they are indeed your decisions; but what I am saying is that I understand.

Anyways back to my story, my mother was barely home; she worked two jobs, and I believe even three at one point. This meant that my siblings (the older ones) watched me. More like bossing me around because I was the youngest. I never really got along too much with them because they picked on me. We all played sports at one time, but that wasn't the case for one year. My sister was the only one cheerleading that year for some after-school program called pop warner. I don't really remember why but one evening, it was just my brother at home and me. Mom had gotten off work and called to tell us that she was headed to the grocery store to pick up my sister and would be home afterward. I remember lying down on the couch, falling asleep, and waking up to my brother on top of me. My mother had this golden furniture at the time coated in cherrywood, I believe, with these big fancy-trimmed pillows with tassels hanging from the four corners. I remember this day like it was yesterday.

The first time I had my innocence taken from me was by my brother. My stomach still turns at the thought of it. He held me down and kissed my face and neck. He caressed my breast, put his hands in my pants, and inserted them inside me. I cried, I yelled, " get off of me" "what are you doing" "stop get off of me" but after what seemed like 2 hours had gone by, my words turned into silent cries. I fought, but it was no use; he was four years older and had at least 60-75 pounds on me. It was hopeless, and right before he pulled down his pants to finish what he had started, my mother walked into the front door. With groceries in her hands, she busted in and caught him in the act. He jumped up so did I.

She immediately started punching and beating on him. Conflicted and shocked, I'm sure, she even yelled at me to go into my room. I sat in that room for a while, crying in the dark, replaying the feeling repeatedly in my head. I don't even think I ate dinner that night. Questions running through my head like, What did I do? Why did he do this to me? Am I in trouble too? Is my mother upset with me too? I remember my mother calling a few people. My stepdad, my grandmother, and my aunt (one of my mother's older sisters, who was also my brother's

Godmother). I remember speaking briefly to my grandmother that night; she was asking me questions about what had happened. I probably repeated that story at least 5-10 times that night. I was so tired that I ended up falling asleep.

I woke up the next morning; my brother wasn't in the house, and my sister had told me that she overheard mom on the phone saying he was living with his father (we all have different dads). My sister still, to this day, doesn't know the full story of what happened that previous night before. My mother made sure I didn't tell her anything, either. I don't ever remember being asked if I was okay. And I was forbidden ever to bring that situation up again. My mom's exact words were, "what goes on in my house stays in my house, and if I hear my business outside of my house, then you will get dealt with ."She always ended her dictatorship statements with a "Do I make myself clear ."So toxic now that I look back on it. I was never offered counseling or therapy. No sexual assault groups or anything.

My mom made sure to use her authority as a parent to keep my lips zipped, locked, and sealed. From everyone. That included my dad and dad's side of the family as well. It's crazy that my mother, who was supposed to protect me no matter what, didn't. This was the moment when everything had changed. This was the moment when my childhood was traumatically stripped away from me, and nobody even cared to ask me if I was okay. This was the moment when the love I had for people (family) changed. This was the moment when I transitioned from an innocent little girl to "That Girl."

Tables turned, and roots began to grow. Unforgiveness. No effective communication. Gossip. Lies. Religion. Broken relationships. Secrets. Betrayal. I was hurt; I was devastated. We never addressed the issue at hand, just walked over them, leaving problems unresolved and giving me a bad taste in my mouth concerning specific individuals. We never came together as a family and discussed how things made one another feel. It was a constant battle between heart and mind for me. My voice was silenced. I was never heard, but I was always told I was disrespectful for having a valid opinion. I was being forced into a silent corner for speaking up about wrongdoings. We argued more than talked, which was the seed planted that would grow for many years.

GOSSIP

If something were to happen in the household where I grew up, we (children) couldn't talk about it. With this said, talking about it is all our parents did. We were told things like, "what happens in my house stays in my house, and if I hear you talking about it, then that's your ASS!"—ever heard of that game Telephone? One person whispers to the person beside them, but when we get to the last person, the initial message never comes back the same. That's how my family was. Aunts, uncles, cousins, and grandparents knew everything, even if it embarrassed us, kids. We were talked about instead of helped. Everyone always had an opinion about someone else, but when it came to their trash, they never wanted to take it out.

LIES & BETRAYAL

Growing up, there were so many family secrets I lost count. Nobody told the truth, people cheated, and my eyes were forced open as a kid to watch. As an adult, I tend to run away from love because it did me no justice as a kid. It's crazy because my mindset and mentality didn't change until this year. Family is supposed to be the closest people to us, but sometimes they are the farthest. Backstabbing became so familiar it was like second nature to those in the generations that came before me. How sick generations suffered because of lack of accountability.

RELIGION

Now, this is a touchy subject. At about the age of 19 is when I began to take my relationship with Christ seriously. I ended up leaving my home church and seeking God on where to go. I ended up visiting a few different churches. None of them were really for me until I was asked to come to a ministry that changed my life forever. It's funny looking back on it now. I had to leave what was familiar to me to grow and grow with God. I used to know him through people but stepping away from people taught me that I didn't know him at all. My grandfather is a well-known bishop that didn't fully practice what he preached. No wonder why my mom was the way she was. Through my relationship with Christ, I've learned how to extend grace, even when I didn't want to. Sometimes we never really know why a person does or doesn't do what we think they should do. When you step out of the storm, you get a clear perspective on what they endured in their lives outside of their relationship with you. My mom isn't just my mom. She is her own person that has gone through her own challenges that negatively impacted her ability to live up to her role as my mother.

BROKEN RELATIONSHIPS

Who knew that one broken relationship would set the tone for all of the relationships in my life? My relationship with my mom was like a rock plummeting into a lake, creating ripples in every other relationship I've tried to develop. Even after being hurt, I tried so hard to mend the relationship between her and me. Until one day, I got fed up. I was the kid and the parent at the same time. But eventually, reaching out to reconcile became draining. You know that old saying, "You could lead a horse to a pail of water, but you can't force him to drink"? That's exactly how I felt. I poured so much energy into mending what I didn't break. And not getting the response that I was hoping for was

just another slap in my face. So, I guess we can add this to my Pandora's box of trauma.

SECRETS

I have to be honest with you guys. I'm not perfect. I've said some things that hurt; I've done some things purposely that bruised. I've even thrown people under the bus to save myself, but it was the defense mechanism that sprouted from those bitter roots. It turns out that hurt people really do hurt people. It's crazy that you cannot like something or someone so much but end up just like them or doing some of the same things you hate. But when you know better, you do better, and once you change how you think about something, the things you think about will change. Perspective is everything, but the first step to living a changed life is forgiving yourself and accepting everything that has happened in its totality.

STRENGTHS

I didn't really know what I was good or strong at until I needed to pull those strengths from deep within. I used to be told as a kid that I talked too much but it turns out that talking is one of my strengths. I now use my voice to write meaningful poetry, or spoken word, about some of the things I've endured in life. Not only does that promote healing in my own life, but it also helps promote healing in others as well, which brings me to my second strength: helping others. See, I've always known that I enjoyed helping others, but it wasn't until adulthood that I realized that helping was one of my strengths. Have you ever heard that scripture that talks about overcoming by the words of your testimony? I turned that into a life motto, and I use my pain to produce purpose. Many people don't know this, but I used to draw as a kid. Drawing turned into painting, and painting turned into makeup. So now I use my face as a canvas to express the beauty that I feel from within. Over the course of four plus years, doing makeup on myself has now trickled into a business, "AmoreAmore" which I now service women everywhere, promoting self confidence in and out of my makeup chair. I've embraced who I am, using my talents and strengths to help people become who they are.

Life is 20% of what happened to you and 80% of how you respond to it. I have not reached my plateau of becoming just yet, but every day I strive to become my better self despite what I endured as a child. Some days are better than most, but every day I choose better even when better didn't choose me. So today, I celebrate my transition from "that girl" to become "her ."Understanding that life is a journey and not a destination. Unmuting my voice to help others find theirs. I am embracing forgiveness and unlearning some toxic traits I picked up in childhood. Understanding that change isn't so much about willpower as it is about why power. I want to leave you all with this quote: "Trauma will always change you, but only you get to say how." Life's experiences will force you into things that you never thought you were capable of doing. I survived 100% of my worst days, and that's something to be proud of. Consistency is key to creating your ideal life despite what you've gone through. And remember, your past is only one chapter, not your whole book.

LETTER TO SELF

Dear Younger Self,

Let me be the first one to apologize to you since you never received one. I am so sorry that you had to endure what you did. I am so sorry that you're scarred by those who were supposed to love you. I want you to know that you will overcome all the dark emotions you've been feeling. I want you to know that you will supersede any and every false presumption ever placed on you. I want you to know that you are an overcomer, and, despite the trauma, you will triumph and give a voice to those who have been silenced. Always remember to put your best foot forward in everything that you do, and remember your past is just that. And it doesn't define you. Continue to stay accountable and intentional as you heal. Continue to be H.O.T. "Honest, open, and transparent". And always remember that you are the flower that blossomed through the concrete. I love you so much and am very proud of who you are becoming.

CHAPTER SIX

The Storm

Daphney Walker

The Cloud lingers but, in a distance, barely noticeable to the naked eye. Where I stand, it is all sunny skies and smooth sailing as so to speak. I am going to college. I have several colleges to choose from. I select a small one. After all, I am a small-town girl who is quiet, shy and reserved. I look forward to it because it is my dream come true. I have worked hard throughout my elementary, junior high, and high school years to achieve my goal of being a high school graduate and college-bound student.

So, when I get my acceptance letters, I really ponder over them. I know I am not ready for the bigger universities I get accepted to. I choose the smaller one in hopes of receiving my education to become a nurse. I dreamed of becoming a nurse all my life. It is what I envision. When I was younger, I played nurse and tended to my dolls. In all fairness, yes, I took them apart but only to see how I could fix them or nurse them back together again, LOL.

My acceptance letter tells me I will start college with a pre-college session that begins in June. And I will start in the fall as a full-time matriculating student. I am fortunate to have received a couple of scholarships, but I will also have to do a work-study program to pay for tuition. But I am eager to get started. My dad tells us we are a dollar short of poverty, and he means it! So, to have the opportunity to go to college is a miracle.

The cloud is approaching but still not apparent to me. I am on the college campus. My parentsand sister have dropped me off. They are equally happy for me. I watch them as they drive away,and it is now that I start feeling a little apprehension, a little fear, but I brush it off. Like so manythings, I have learned to brush off in my life. Face whatever it is you must face and tread onward. Don't forget your Mask. You must wear it at all times. Never let anyone know how you feel. My mother taught us that we are not to show displeasure. Her favorite expression is "get mad, get glad"; it's your choice. I hear the expression countless times, especially after getting a beating. I just want to be mad and believe I have every right to be mad. But no, my mother tickles your knees or does something to make you laugh and/or smile. You really cannot stay "mad" long. The word mad is too strong a word, so my mother says you cannot say the word mad, but you are allowed to say the word angry.

The Mask covers all the displeasure you are feeling. Just keep smiling, and the whole world smiles with you. I consider the Mask I am taught to wear. I think of Maya Angelou's poem, "The Mask," which she adapted from a poem written by Paul Laurence Dunbar back in 1896 called "We Wear the Mask." I am brought to an awareness that my mother has been taught to wear the Mask, as was her mother. I realize the Mask goes as far back as slavery days. It makes sense to me now, as slaves could not show their displeasure without receiving some type of reprimand from their master. A slave would have to take whatever was given to him, smile, and pretend that all was well. My mother taught us that to succeed in life, you must learn to get along with the white man. She would say you will have to work with the white man and need to learn how to act around the white man. My mother taught us that you will work three times harder than the white man.

Sometimes life has a way of giving you experiences that make your mother's teachings understandable. Life will also give you experiences you are unprepared for in any way, shape, or form. Life can be so unpredictable. I grew up having dreams, visions, and desires, and I believe I will attain them. But I am thinking... This is it; it is finally happening. I am all of 17 years old and maturing. I smell the sweet aroma of success, having completed high school and going onto college. I am going to start my journey to becoming a nurse. I am beginning a new chapter of my life. I am going forward with full force and all the energy I can muster. I am happy and enthusiastic about the up-and-coming college experience.

As I settle into my dorm room, there is not much to do as my stay will only be for six weeks, and then I will return home and prepare to come back for the fall semester. I do take the time to say a prayer, which is just talking to God. I do not expect an answer as I have been taught; he sits high and looks low. I have been talking to God since I was a child. I complained, and I did vent a lot. On this day, I thank God and tell Him of my gratitude that I have made it this far. I know my dream is coming to fruition. I also take time to make a note to myself. Self, try to be outgoing and not your shy, timid, reserved self. I reflect on a Bible verse that says, if you are going to make friends, you must show yourself friendly. Making friends is something I have difficulty doing. I do not like being around many people and prefer to stay alone. I find people can be a bit overwhelming. I know I must gather the courage to do so and face this new part of my journey. If not, I will face it alone.

It is time… I have a list of events I must attend that are prepared for me. The first event is my introduction to college. I have a meeting with the admissions director. I take the school map to find where I need to go to get to the admissions director's office. I am at his office at the appointed time. I knock on the door and wait for his invitation to enter. The admissions director says, "come in." I enter the office to see a white man short in stature sitting in his chair in front of his desk, motioning me to have a seat. So, I do. I say hello. I wait to hear his welcome speech as he fumbles through some papers. Well, I assume it is why I am here in the admissions director's office, a welcome speech, right? There is no one else in the room. It is just the admissions director and me. I am getting nervous and a little jittery. I do not see a smile or any remote sign on the admissions director's face that he is glad to meet me. But I patiently wait for him to say what he has to say.

The admissions director proceeded to tell me they took my application out of the trash because of something called "affirmative action." I clearly am not prepared to hear the words coming out of his mouth right now. I admit I went numb after hearing my application taken out of the trash. Who says such a thing? Affirmative action supposedly affords me an opportunity to go to college. I am thinking; in my mind, I am trying to process his words. I am at a loss for words. Finally, I do come to my senses, and I am thinking and probably screaming from someplace inside of myself that I have worked hard and achieved good grades. But all I can think to say is thank you for this opportunity. That is it. In one fell swoop, I am deflated. There is one thing I know: this man, this admissions director, does not know me. I think if this is their way of discouraging me, well, they have another thing coming. Trash or no trash, I am a determined soul. Neither do I believe that I did not earn the right to attend this college. But it is disheartening, to say the least. The cloud that has been in the distance is now upon me as I am writhing with anger. But, I put on the Mask I had been taught to wear and smiled as I left his office. He may have said a thousand other words, but that is all I hear for the day and all that I remember for that day.

There are other events/gatherings for us students. So that we can get to know one another, it is a trying time for me as I am more of an introvert than an extrovert. But I attend the gatherings with hopes of making friends. Our group is small, and all of us are African American. I must suppose that is primarily because we are all here because of Affirmative Action and that they received the same reception I did from the admissions director. But no one really mentioned their engagements with the admissions director. I am too embarrassed to talk about my experience. I cannot believe someone of authority said something demeaning to me. This cloud within me is shading me with darkness and some gloom. I am beginning to feel as though things are amiss.

At our first welcoming event, we introduced ourselves to one another. I do feel like I am on my own now. I try my best at small talk. I remember one boy talking with me, and he says something that makes me think we are still in high school. I feel it is immature of him to say what he said. The girls seem nice enough, and a couple of them seem more "street-wise" than not, to put it politely, even more than I can imagine them to be at our age. We also have a black counselor who is approximately thirty-five years old. I am sure the black counselor is there to provide us with some affiliation that helps us to acclimate to the college we are attending. After all, the college campus is predominantly white.

College life is difficult for me. The time is about two weeks in. I have boys asking me if I am a virgin. They tell me they would be happy to show me the ropes, so to speak. I let them know what they don't know; they'll never know. The boys always let me know who is doing what and with whom. They just offer this information without me asking. I let them know I could care less. I am amazed that they speak so freely of their sexual escapades. The girls are just as bad. The girls sit around talking about their sexual escapades. Me, I am looking and feeling clueless. I have absolutely nothing to boast about. They are bragging about their sexual escapades because it makes them feel like they are grown women. So, after telling their stories, they ask, Daphney, what about you? I say, "I have to go, I have something to do, and I must go and sweep my dorm room floor or something." Anything to get out of there. I intend to hold onto my virginity until marriage, per my biblical teachings. Teachings that teach you about treating your body like a temple and that a young lady's body is sacred and of value. My belief is that once you meet the right man and enter holy matrimony, then sexual intimacy follows. It is my belief, and I am sticking to it. I do not like being hounded by boys at all. I find it quite distressing, and I find myself at the brunt of many students' conversations. The boys act offended when I refuse their advances.

Because of the way I was raised, I believed in having morals and standards. Therefore, I stood my ground when it came to the boys. But at some point, I notice they treat me differently from the girls who are "putting it out there." They have respect for me. It is evident when they come to me and tell me that one of the boys says he slept with me, and they tell me they know it was a lie because they knew I did not sleep with anyone. I told the boys to let the boy know that he was a liar, and the next time he says something like that, he should tell everyone he had a dream.

One evening, I am in my dorm room listening to my little white radio and reading a book. I heard a knock at my door. When I opened the door, one of the girls from my group was standing there. She told me our counselor was having a party in his dorm room. She said the counselor sent her as he wanted me to join them. I told her I would come after I got ready for the party, which meant nothing fancy, just a change of clothes (LOL). I throw on a sweatshirt and baggy pants. Because I am not fond of cafeteria food, I lost some weight. I really did not have many clothes to choose from.

I head out to my counselor's dorm room. When I went inside, there were at least six of us from our small group of black pre-college students. It seems as if I am not here very long, maybe all of ten minutes, before they all start leaving. Like, all at once. I think, why are they leaving, and I just arrived? It is supposed to be a party, and it is early yet. It is about nine o'clock p.m. I know students party later than this. But I have no idea how long the other students were there before I arrived. Clouds are moving in, clouds of discomfort and uncertainty.

My counselor is talking to me. At the same time, he pours into a glass some Wild Irish Rose, an alcoholic beverage. I let him know I do not drink. I know in my mind; I am not going to drink it. So, I look at the glass and let it sit. My counselor decides to get comfortable and lays across his bed. I do not know why I feel afraid just to leave. I think I may offend him by leaving too soon. Now, I am thinking I must do something. I think it put him to sleep. So, I speak to him in a monotone voice deliberately about anything and everything until he falls asleep. I creep out the door for fear of waking him. I realize on my walk back to my dorm room that it is foolish of me to think my counselor is trying to get me drunk so he can take advantage of me. I have heard that boys try to get a girl drunk to take advantage of her, but my counselor is a grown man, to me, at thirty-five years old. I was not allowed to go to parties when I was growing up.

My parents were strict. I lead a very sheltered life. I do not know what to think or what to expect. I really do not know what to make of it all. So, once at my dorm room, I prepare for bed. I climb into my bed and lay my head to rest, yet I find I still have thoughts about what took place. I still have questions about why the students left me. The next day comes, and I do not think much of the day before. I am busy with the things that are planned for our day. I do not speak to anyone about what happened. Neither do I question anybody about why they left the party. I am too embarrassed because I think I might be trying to make something out of nothing. After all, nothing happened. It was all in my head. Later in the evening, I am in my dorm room, and I get a knock at the door. I answered, and again, it was the same girl telling me my counselor was having another party and was asking for me to come. I agree to come. I pull myself together. It is not unusual for impromptu parties to pop up on a college campus. It does not take much for a party to happen. College students can find a reason to party, any reason. Oh, look, it stopped raining, let's have a party. So, I cannot say that I am questioning the fact that there is another party.

I remember the walk to my counselor's room because I had a conversation with myself. I guess all kinds of missiles are going off in my head because of yesterday's experience with the counselor. There may be a cloud of doom and gloom lurking about, but I do not recognize it. I have questions about why students would leave or why the counselor would pour me a drink. I am thinking, what if this counselor wants to have sex with me. I'm thinking, no, he's a grown man, he's 35 years old, what would he want with a 17-year-old girl. I was trying to use reason and/or logic to have things make sense to me. I even reminded myself that a grown man would ask you if he wants to have sex with you. I think if my counselor does ask, I will politely tell him no, as that is what a mature woman does.

But I assure you, I am not convinced that a grown man will ask to have sex with me. I can also assure you I am not as grown as I think I am at 17 years old. I cannot begin to fathom why this scenario was even playing out in my head. So, I made up my mind as to what I will do if my counselor wanted to have sex with me. I will tell him NO as I am saving myself for marriage. Although I think my thoughts are absurd and foolish because what grown man is interested in me? I am a "plain jane," as so to speak. I am timid, shy, and much prefer to stay to myself.

My clothes are baggy and hang off my body. Especially now since I do not find the cafeteria food appetizing. I do not wear makeup, and my hair is in braids. I neither have the time nor money to look glamorous. I am not the type of girl to throw myself at the boys or a grown man, for that matter. I know I want to make friends, and I think this is my opportunity to do so. I am hopeful I will be mingling with everyone at the party. I was in the counselor's room, and it's more of a double dorm room, so he does have some space. There are the familiar faces of the same pre-college students from the evening before who are there. I am welcomed into the room but just as mysteriously as the evening before, everyone, and I mean everyone, leaves all at once. I am now suspicious and confused. What is going on? I am ready to leave now, at once, immediately. The clouds are churning, darkening as I am more apprehensive now than ever before.

Could there be something up, something devious, or is it me? So, I turned to walk away or maybe even run away because now, at that moment, something did not feel right. No, this is wrong. Something is truly suspicious. But the counselor is slick. He had already positioned himself between me and the door. I am thinking, what must I do to get out the door? I look towards the door, and all I can see is the counselor looming and towering over me so much that the door is just about hidden from my sight. I do the only thing I can think of, which is to proclaim to the counselor that I am leaving as well, in what I thought was my most convincing voice. I could feel it though in my belly; in my innards, there is a shaking, a rumbling of sorts. My Mask is on, and I am not about to show the fear and anxiety I am experiencing while I battle with my brain to keep my wits about me.

The counselor does not move away from the door as I thought he would. He opens his mouth to say to me this one sentence, "How do you feel about rape?". I am truly confused, rape? What? My mind is reeling, trying to comprehend if the counselor is joking with me or not. Of course, this is not the scenario I practiced in my head. It is the farthest thing from my mind. I reply, "what do you mean? I have no idea; what do you mean?" Then I see him whip something out of his pocket that looks like a blur of a shiny medal. I see it as it unfolds itself! It is a jack-knife! And swifter than I can think, move, and/or scream, the cold, sharp blade of it is upon my throat. I am horrified. At that moment, all I could think was, God help me. Say a prayer, simple but direct, silent but earnest; God help me! I feel the weight and the pressure of the counselor's body pushing me back onto the bed. I hit the bed with a jolt. The blade is still at my neck, and I dare not take too deep of a breath. I dare not breathe. I dare not... I feel him maneuvering my clothes. I feel him like a dead weight lying on me. He is heavy, too heavy. My breaths are shallow and almost nonexistent. The weight, the pressure, and the heaviness make me feel like I can't breathe.

The blade at my throat makes me think, don't move, don't dare move. I feel as though my body wants to shutter and quake at the horror of what is happening to me. How is this even happening to me? How is this possible? Moan silently, whimper silently, tremble silently, scream silently as fear grips me. Fear envelopes me and covers me like a shroud. The storm has encroached upon me with fear and rage. I am afraid as thoughts of life and death go through my head. I cannot breathe. I am lightheaded. He presses himself into me with a force, and I experience a searing, piercing pain. My screams are stifled by the fear of making a sound, the weight of him, and the weight of the blade pressing into my throat. It hurts so deeply to my utmost core. I am physically trying to reject him but cannot. He is forceful and cruel. I have no choice, and I have no voice. My heart is crushed.

Although I can feel the pain, I am trapped, and my screams are trapped. Somehow, those screams are captured and held internally. I cannot let them out. Wear the Mask. Do not let him know what I am feeling inside. No telling what will happen if I let it all out. I no longer want to be here. It is too excruciating to bare. But all at once, I find myself floating. Did I die? I am in the corner of the ceiling, and I am looking down at what is going on. I see what is happening to my body. To me, I am having what is like an out-of-body experience. I see him on top of me doing his dastardly deed. I see myself lying motionless as it is the only way I think I can survive. Here I am wafting above, watching as he continues to rape me, as he violates me and takes my most precious gift. I am impervious to the forceful, painful act of it all. At this moment, I realize he has the body, but he does not have "ME." "ME" is the life and essence of that body. "ME" is the spirit and soul of that body.

The counselor will never have, could never have "ME." I know I am more than just my body. I know I own the essence, the soul of me. At this point, I know my soul, my spirit, is separate from my body but housed in my body. It makes a difference to me. I am young, I am innocent, and I have no idea anyone could be so brutal, be so cruel to me. At this moment, it means everything to me. Looking down at my body and not allowing myself to feel in that moment keeps me from moving, keeps me from screaming, it just keeps me.

I liken the experience to my body being like a house, and it is ravaged by a storm. The damage is done. The shutters are torn away. The roof is partially attached, and there is still a foundation. The house can still stand but needs major repairs. But a house cannot repair itself. When he is done, he lets me go. No words needed, no nod of the head, nothing. Just the removal of the blade from my throat is acknowledgement enough. I cannot make eye contact. I cannot look at him. I cannot speak. I am trying to aright my clothing as I rush out the door. I am shaking, battered, and disgusted. I am disgusted with him. I am disgusted with myself. I know I look a mess. I don't care. I am hurrying, running in a panic to get to my dorm room. At the same time, I am thinking. I cannot wrap my head around the fact that the counselor has raped me. That I have been raped. The question in my head is, why did he do this? Why? Why? Why? God, why??? "Could all the students be in on it? Why did they leave?". Too many questions to ask. I am lost in the recesses of my mind as I drift off into a deep abyss.

I am alone. Feeling like I am a discarded dirty dish rag. He dispenses of me like I am nothing. I cannot process or fathom

how someone can do such a horrendous act. The experience
leaves me numb and unfeeling. I try to clean up, but there is not
enough showering or scrubbing in the world to clean up the
dirty, filthy feeling I feel. I cry and sob while the tears flow until
they cannot flow anymore. If it is not a stream of tears, it is a
river of tears I cry. I move and walk around but with habitual
movements. It is like following a script and I do what I normally
do. Wear my Mask. But I am by no means normal. My mind is
overtaken with thoughts about what has happened and why it
has happened. I never come to a logical, reasonable, viable
conclusion.

  Nothing makes sense. I carry the weight of it in silence. I
am sick to my heart, my mind, and my soul. My head aches and
my stomach churns as I think of it. I am at a loss for words. I am
at a loss… I lost my virginity. No! My virginity was ripped and
scathingly torn from me in a way I never imagined or intended
to happen! It is not supposed to happen like this!. It is not what
I envisioned for myself. I recognize I have been dealt a blow like
none other in my life. I am tainted, I am spoiled, I am worn, and
I do not know what it will take to recover. There is a grieving
period and a time to process with any loss. But, not having gone
through something like this ever before, I have no idea what
grieving and processing looks like or should look like, for that
matter. I do what I am taught to do anytime I experience pain

or any type of suffering, and that is to deal with it. It is to suffer in silence and to pull myself together. I must wear the mask, wear a fake smile, to continue like nothing is wrong; it is to continue. I do not let my emotions or feelings show, which at times is near impossible.

I confide in the one girl who comes to my dorm room on both nights and who beckons me to come to the counselor's room. She is the closest person I would have poised myself to name as a friend. I look her in the eye as I tell her what the counselor did to me. I can never forget the blank deer in the headlights stare she gives back to me. Her lips do not move, and she has no response for me. What can I expect her to say? Is she in on it? Are they all in on it??? It appears that way. I am not close to any of the students. I rather be by myself even though I do try to make friends.

I think about who to tell. I think about my parents. I determine I cannot tell anyone. I believe in my heart of hearts that if I tell my parents, or if they find out, it will kill them. I fear they will also think the worst of me. Somehow, I am blaming myself for being raped by the counselor. It isn't about getting angry or mad at someone; it is about pushing through it right now. I know I am upset with the counselor and really do not know what to do, what to think or how to act. I still must see him every day and interact with him on some level. It is unsettling to my very being. He is a constant reminder of the most horrible moment in my life. I cannot look at him. My eyes are always cast down. In hopes, he is unable to read my feelings or my thoughts in some way. After all, it is my fault for putting myself in that kind of predicament, isn't it? At least, that is what I think people will say.

There is not a day that goes by that I do not feel alone. I feel as though no one can understand. I feel they will blame me as I blame myself. I blame myself for being innocent and naïve. I blame myself for believing in and trusting in people. Yes, it hurts, it hurts so very bad. Like someone rakes your heart, your soul, your very being over hot coals. As hard as it is, life goes on. I return home from the pre-college program for about a month before having to go back to college for the real deal. I am quiet, I am pensive, and I am trying to prepare myself for the upcoming school year. I do not feel like I have any other options as there is no Plan B. Plan A is what I know and I worked so hard to achieve. Why would I think of doing anything differently? So, hide my feelings, I must. My parents cannot catch onto anything being amiss. The storm clouds continue to brew even after the storm.

LETTER TO SELF

Dear Daphney,

Although you may feel absolutely devasted by the turn of events that happened when you started college, it is imperative that you keep your focus on what is bright and lovely in your life. I know it seems life has dealt you a blow that has knocked you down into the abyss. The darkness is so intense that it makes you feel like you are covered with a shroud. The sadness you feel is overwhelming, and the hopelessness makes you feel like you cannot live or you should not live. Don't stay in the pain and grief of what has happened for too long. Sometimes you must seek the things that bring you solace. You know, like going to the park, sitting next to the water, and watching the sunrises and sunsets. Take time to play some of your favorite tunes that uplift and inspire you. Like, Earth, Wind & Fire's "Keep Your Head To The Sky".

Remember to say your prayers and that God is with you through it all. Seek God with all your heart, mind, and soul. Know that God loves you very, very much and He knows and feels your pain, grief and sorrow. Jesus experienced trauma so He is able to identify with the myriad of emotions you are experiencing. Hold on to His nail scarred hands and know He too has suffered. The Mask is useful up to a point. At some point, you must process what has happened and not continue to internalize it all. Most importantly, remember to forgive. It may seem easier to forgive others, but please remember to forgive yourself and stop blaming yourself. Do not let your self-esteem, self-confidence, and self-love be damaged by it all. Know that you are valuable, you are worthy, and you are loved. You must love yourself and remember self-sacrifice does not mean you love yourself less.

Admit this to yourself; you do not know what the future holds. Say it! I do not know what the future holds. Now believe for the bright and beautiful to come out as you persevere with all your heart and all your might. Maintain your belief in God, continue in hope no matter how hopeless the situation feels, act by faith and love with the Love of God. All these things, hope, faith, and love, are within you. They are seeds that have been planted within you through biblical teachings. Life throws fertilizer on those seeds. The fertilizer and the dung are necessary for the process. No matter how unpleasant. The process allows you to achieve the growth that is necessary to become the beautiful, strong, courageous woman you are. The future is brighter than you think.

Love,

Daphney

P.S. The sun does come out tomorrow. It is 1994 and I am outside with the sunny and blue sky above me. I have my cap and gown on. So much has happened since the event, since the story I spoke of. I can say with God's help I am still standing today. I am smiling as my name is called by the college dean, Daphney Arlene Gibson-Walker. I begin my march onward like a Christian soldier. I ascend up the stairs and march across the stage. I stop to receive my diploma that signifies I earned my Bachelor of Science in Nursing degree. I am ecstatic and I am happy. It is my dream come true.

CHAPTER SEVEN

Pieces Of Me

B. Williams

September 3 was the day for me. So many people have many different dates they recall and can explain in precise detail the events of that day for many reasons—the birth of a child, new jobs, new opportunities, and so forth. For me, this day meant so much more. My grandmother and my youngest brother share the same birthday, September 3. Little did I know this day would be a major turning point for the rest of my life.

I can remember going to the Dover Mall with my mother. As soon as she pulls into the mall parking lot, my phone pings. "Hey, I'm back in town; what's up" this text was coming from a fling—a real nice, casual guy by the name of Mel. I had met up with him on a few occasions for a couple of months at this point. I look over to my mom, and she says, "what's wrong" I respond, "Mel just hit me up after going MIA for a couple of weeks",," Not sure if this is something I really want to do." At the time, I was just tired and wasn't in the mood to entertain or be around anyone. If I had followed my gut instincts and listened to my inner consciousness, I would have saved myself from a lot of pain.

My mother and I walk into the mall. I recall going into DEBS. It was a clothing store for young women. You could go in there and find just about anything from casual attire to formal wear. I found this maroon and black dress and some nice black heels to go along with it. I wanted to match the décor colors that they were using for my grandmother's party, so I tried to get as close to it as possible with the chosen dress colors. While shopping, I still couldn't get the thought out of my head. "What should I do"? Should I go, should I just stay home? I am such a people pleaser and just felt like I had to show my face.

Instead of leaving him wondering for the rest of the day, I text back and say, "I can come through, but I won't be staying long." Something felt completely off, but I felt okay with being really open about my plans with him for the evening. He responds, "Okay, cool. He stated he would text me closer to when he was on his way to me. Another red flag that I unfortunately ignored. Every time we met up, I always took myself. I never put myself in a situation to be without transportation, a situation I still regret to this day.

My mom and I ended up leaving the mall and spent the rest of the day with the kids doing family things. We cooked, cleaned, and got our party outfits situated to ensure they fit for the big day. Finally, mom and I sat down, discussed more party details, and talked about how we couldn't wait to see how surprised my grandmother was with this surprise party. As I was getting ready to spend the evening with Mel, I was still tossing the idea around of not going at all. Eventually, I got in the shower to get ready for the evening. I recall throwing on a t-shirt and some black shorts. I remember smelling the warm summer rain in the air. It was so humid and dreary outside. The clouds filled the sky with a thick covering as if they knew what was getting ready to happen.

Soon enough, my phone pings again. It's MEL! Requesting the address to pick me up. I give him the address, still very much leery about even going out with him. It was almost like a gut instinct telling me not to go out with him. A gut instinct I should've followed! I get another text saying, "yo, I'm outside." I remember hearing the engine roaring like a lion on his gold Tahoe. I proceed to walk out to get into his truck. On the way to his home, we briefly discussed him and his most recent trip back home to Virginia. The ride seemed so long, passing all the late-night food spots. The ride that should've been about 5 minutes seemed like 15.

Once we pulled up to his spot, I noticed the downstairs was lit up like a Christmas tree. I recall asking if he had his kids with him, and he responded, "no." I understood he lived there alone, so I was shocked to see almost what seemed like all of the lights on. Once we walk in, I notice a man with dreads and a woman also in the kitchen. They are drinking liquor and taking shots. Mel tried to get me to drink, but I declined because I didn't like liquor. I recall him saying, "here, yo, take the shot" I reply with a "Nah, I'm good."

I felt slightly uncomfortable as he hadn't told me he had company at home. He hadn't disclosed any of that at all to me throughout our text. However, seeing another female there had me feeling slightly relieved. Cory, the cousin, and Angel, the other female, stay downstairs, and Mel and I head upstairs to the room. Once in the room, we start kissing, and one thing leads to another. He begins giving me oral. Maybe after about 5 minutes, I notice a light in the room. Mind you; the room was pitch dark the whole time. I look over, and someone is peeping into the room. I tell Mel to watch out so that I can cover myself up. Before I knew it, Mel said, "you good" keep going. I say, "excuse me; no, someone else is in here." That's when the nightmare began. That's the point where the old me was lost forever.

Mel rolls me over and begins to penetrate me from behind at this point. I don't know how but Cory ends up in front of me, shoving his penis in my mouth. The weight and size of those guys are crazy. I felt so overpowered. I recall saying no, yelling no, and asking them to stop. After what felt like an hour, I became numb. I can remember seeing myself standing in a corner, just looking down at my own body and not being able to help. I recall being scared, closing my eyes, and praying to God to get me back to my children. I didn't care how he got me back to them, but I needed to get back to my kids.

A few moments later, a THIRD guy enters the room. By this point, I am literally numb. They are moving me from position to position, and I just feel dead. I am so heavily assaulted that I start bleeding from my vagina. I remember hearing one of them say, "yo man, she's bleeding." The third guy, the older guy, was disgusting. I recall getting a glimpse of his face; he had to be in this late 50's. I couldn't help to think, "What if this was your daughter? Granddaughter? Niece"?

After more time, they began to call themselves the wolf pack. They began to howl and bite me. My back, legs, and inner thighs receive bite marks. As I continue to lay there, I just think I have to survive and do what they want to get back to my kids. Eventually, the attack was over. They threw a warm wet washcloth at me and told me to clean myself up. I recall seeing my blood smeared on the nude linens like jelly being spread on bread. I recall thinking, "if the cops come, they will have evidence." Surprisingly, Mel takes me back home. On the way,

I say to him, "I pray no one ever hurts your daughters the way you hurt me."

On September 3, my brother's birthday, I spent that whole entire day in and out of the shower and tub. I was showering, soaking, showering, soaking. I stayed away and was secluded from my family the entire day. I felt so dirty, yet after bathing all day, I was technically clean. Eventually, I told my mother. She calls my dad, and he comes to town with my cousin. I recall my 4'11 mother walking up to that house, knocking on the door, and looking for Mel. A female answered but not the female from the night before. I recall hearing my mom yelling, looking for him. Before arriving at the house, my mother called the police to report the incident. While there, 911 pulls up to the residence. The officer tells my mom to take me to the station to make an official report. I got to the station, made an official report, and provided them with all the details. They tell us because I showered, that evidence was probably long gone. The police department didn't even attempt to have a rape kit done. At that point, an overwhelming feeling of defeat and guilt rested on me like a thousand-pound weight.

I knew I couldn't have been their first. From how easily and well executed it was, I feel like I wasn't the only person to be victimized by them. Eventually, my mom took me on her own to Bay Health to be examined; as we thought, there was no evidence. The only thing that they could prove was that "rough intercourse happened." We argued with our local police officer. We then found out that Corey, the cousin's father-in-law was a high-ranked police officer. The case was eventually thrown out for lack of evidence. I again felt defeated. I felt like they didn't believe me. It was heartbreaking.

I lost friends behind this; I went to school and was really close with their niece. My cousin stopped talking to me because she was close friends with one of the men. It was a real turning point for me. Everything seemed so dark, almost as if I were in a blacked-out tunnel and couldn't find my way out. Although I had so much love and support from my family, I felt so alone. September 3 is a day I'll never forget. The day of my own personal transition.

LETTER TO SELF

Hello Little B,

Please know you are worth it; you are enough and beautiful. You deserve all things good in life. Love yourself more than anything. Develop healthy ways to release stress, to cope with life; you can do it, baby girl! Believe in yourself even when the world does not. Venture and see the beautiful world. There is so much out here to see and to grasp. Take it all in. You may fall, but you CAN NOT, and you WILL NOT stay there. Get up. Restart and try again. When you get back up, you will be stronger and wiser. Remember, there is a lesson to learn in every piece of life. Never stop learning, never stop growing. Don't be afraid to feel. Feel all of those emotions and express each one of them – healthy ways only, though ☺.

Keep the faith. You will find peace in listening to Yolanda Adams (Open My Heart) and Smokie Norful (I Need You Now). Believe in God. Even in your darkest moments – pray, pray, and more prayer. Speak life into yourself and everyone around you. Believe God would never leave you nor forsake you.

Make your boundaries and make others follow them if they cannot LEAVE THEM!

Little B – you are golden baby!

CHAPTER EIGHT

Don't Let Your Situation Change Your Revelation

Eneri

I grew up in the city... tall buildings, row homes, lots of people, and fast traffic. 30th Diamond... I remember saying that when people would ask me where I was from. My row home stood tall, almost halfway up the block. There was always a lot of noise outside. I remember seeing many people and consistently wondering what each person was thinking in their mind and what they had going on in their lives. My house always seemed to stand out from the other houses on the block. It was a different color, and we had many beautiful plants out front. We were the only house on the block with a front bench. A few steps led up to the front door of my childhood home. I often sat on these steps to watch people and cars go by. Walking through the front door of my home, I immediately stepped into a beautiful corridor. 6-7 silver metal mailboxes were to the right on the wall, and the floor had a designer porch rug on it. There was a second door that needed to be passed to have access to the rest of the home. I used to get so mad when this door shut behind me if I forgot my key. It locked automatically, and I would always forget to put the stopper down.

I remember walking through a third door to the right to access the first-floor apartment. This was our primary living area for most of my young life. It was my favorite apartment in the whole building. It had white tile floors, white brick wallpaper around the bottom half of the wall, and big mirrors around the top part of the walls. There was this big leather cream couch in the living room that my siblings and I used to sleep on from time to time. The dining room felt like a room that belonged in a castle. It had a big conference glass table that could seat approximately eight people—black trimming along the side of this king's table ☺. The dining room had two big, long windows in it that allowed you to look out front into the streets. I loved this room. It always felt so peaceful and close to the exit of the house. I remember my dad hung our Christmas cross in the middle of this room between the windows during Christmas time. He stated, "Jesus didn't die on a tree, so we will hang and decorate a cross."

Each room was connected to another on the first floor. One long apartment. Our kitchen was a modern styled kitchen, and there were two bedrooms with one luxurious bathroom. My dad added an addition to the second bedroom in the back of the house. This was the award-winning room because he installed a light blue full-size jacuzzi in the middle of the floor with big mirrors. The floors were made of beautiful marble, and he installed a handmade altar with a fireplace. That was where he kept his bible and pictures of people he loved or wanted to pray for. This room was unique. My dad didn't let my mom sleep in it often. He stated the room was for him, and she could have her own space out front on the couch.

Upstairs were two floors in the home. We had a 2nd-floor front and second-floor rear, consisting of two individualized apartments that my dad designed and built himself. The third floor was one long apartment that mirrored the first floor's layout style. However, it wasn't as luxurious as the first floor. Me and my three older siblings stayed on this floor. It had three bedrooms, a kitchen, and a bathroom. My older sister and I shared the front room, and my brothers had their own room. We were unsupervised and told all our friends that we had our own apartment. I enjoyed having my own space unsupervised with my siblings for a long time.

However, I later began to regret that. On this floor is where my whole life changed forever. I remember I was somewhere between the age of 9 and 11 years old. It was a sunny day, and I was playing outside the house on the steps. I remember Dutch riding his bike and asking me where my brother Isaiah was. I responded, "he is in the house somewhere." Dutch asked me if I could go get my brother out of the house. As I ran into the house to search for my brother, Dutch followed me into the house. We walked up the stairs to the third floor. The sunlight was shining through the windows of the rooms. It was quiet, and I didn't see anyone upstairs. I remember checking in Sal's room to see if Isaiah was in there, but it was empty. I remember Dutch standing behind me and asking me where everyone was. I said I didn't know. He blocked the entrance to Sal's room as I tried to walk out. He slowly started walking towards me. He asked me if I had ever had sex before. I asked him what that was. He smiled and said, "you never had sex before; you don't know what sex means." I said, "no." I became scared and confused because I didn't know what sex meant.

He slowly approached me and started rubbing my face. He said, "let me show you." He told me to lay on the bed, and then he took my shorts off. I remember feeling very scared because I didn't know what was happening. I remember my hands being clenched tight up to my chest. He said, "it's going to be okay; you don't have to be scared." I remember my head was turned to the right side. I was staring at the mattress, and he got on top of me. He kissed me on my face and told me I was pretty. I remember his kisses felt disgusting, and I started to feel sick. I remember he penetrated me, thinking this was the worst pain in the world and why someone would do this. I started crying and said, "please get off of me." I tried to lean up, and he pushed me back down. I remember he said he was almost done.

As he penetrated me, I remember crying and saying, please stop. I remember saying help in a moderate tone, but he put his hand over my mouth and said shhh. I remember staring at the mattress more, hoping he would be done soon. I think it lasted for a few minutes. Finally, I remember him getting off the top of me and saying oh my God, you're bleeding. I sat up while still on the bed, and I looked down and saw a lot of blood. I said, "what is that? Why am I bleeding (in shock)? He smiled and said, "I popped your cherry. Congratulations, you're a woman now". I stared at him, confused with tears. He said, "it will be okay." He told me not to tell anyone because we would get in trouble for messing up the mattress if I did. He said if I told anyone, he would say it was all my fault.

[That was the start of the longest summer of my life]

I remember playing with my friends at the park, and Dutch rode by on his bike. It was sunny outside, and a small number of kids were on the playground. He smiled at me and told me to come here. I didn't move, and he rode over to me. He told me he wanted to walk with me somewhere. I told him I didn't want to go. He said, "you don't have a choice." He asked me if I had told anyone about what happened (he stopped smiling and began to frown). I said, "no." He said, "good." When I didn't move, he put a knife to my side and said walk with me. I immediately started walking. We walked for about 3 minutes and arrived at this row home on 33rd street... not too far from the bus depot. He told me to go up the steps, and he followed me.

I remember being scared and thinking, "oh my God"... "what am I going to do if what happened the last time happens again"?. I thought to myself, "what if more people were inside"?... "What if they hurt me"? I remember thinking Oh My God, he will probably kill me. I kept thinking that if I cooperated, maybe he would let me live. He took me into this back room and forced me to go down on him. I remember the room being empty, with hardwood floors, no furniture, and no shades/blinds. Light came in the window, drugs on the floor, corner store bags on the floor, trash on the floor, and a bowl that looked like someone had left old milk in it.

As he sat on the floor, he grabbed the back of my head and forced my mouth on his penis. I remember me saying, trying to talk, asking why he is doing this to me. He told me to shut up and just move my head up and down. I guess I wasn't doing what he wanted me to do because he then put the knife down and grabbed my head with two hands. He forced my head down on him. I remember vomiting, and he gave me the blue bowl with old milk in it to spit up in. I remember me thinking this is my chance to run. He didn't have the knife, and his pants were down, so it would be hard for him to run after me. I got up after throwing up and ran out of the room to find my way out of the house. I remember passing a bathroom to my right and running straight into another door that led to another room. I saw a dark skin woman lying on a mattress in the room. I remember thinking, "is she dead, or is she high on drugs." Dutch stood at the doorway of the room and said, "get out of my mom's room, get away from my mom." I ran down the steps and out the front of the house. I ran home crying.

[Later that summer]

I remember walking up Diamond street between 32nd and 33rd. There was an abandoned house to the right, down a small side block. I remember walking through the block and passing this house without paying it too much attention. Dutch rode past me on the bike and smiled. He winked at me. I remember my heart feeling like it had stopped beating. I tried not to make eye contact and thought about running back home, but my feet wouldn't move. He made a U-turn on his bike and came towards me. I remember saying to myself, "run," but thinking about what bad things could happen if I ran. He said, "what's up" I didn't say anything. He said, "you can't hear me talking to you." I remember standing very still, staring at the ground and debating what to do. I remember him looking around, grabbing me by the back of my neck, and saying, "say something." I remember him grabbing me and the pain making my shoulders clinch upwards. He never let go of my neck and dropped his bike on the ground.

He pushed me towards the abandoned house and forced me up two stairs. I remember looking around for neighbors. I remember seeing people sitting on the steps outside of the houses. Nobody said anything to him. I wasn't sure if anyone noticed. I remember my chest feeling very tight and saying, ouch, you're hurting my neck. He ignored my comments and said you know this is my house, right. He pushed me into the house and pulled out a big black gun.

I immediately stared at the gun and started walking backward. He walked closer to me and put the gun to my head. He told me I want you to do the same thing you did the last time. I didn't say anything but just stared at the gun. I remember hearing his belt unbuckle from his pants and his pants hitting the floor. He kept the gun on the top of my head and grabbed the back of my head with his left hand. I remember him grabbing the back of my head with his left hand and forcing my head toward his genital area. I remember cooperating more this time than the other time. I remember tears falling down my face but being careful not to upset him too much because I thought he would shoot me.

[Fourth Encounter]

I was walking down the street on Lehigh Avenue between 31st and 33rd street. I don't remember where I was going, but I was walking in the direction of the crab shack. Dutch rode past me on his bike and looked at me. I remember it was light outside when I saw him. My mind went blank as he rode up the street. I remember making a U-turn and cutting through the cemetery to go home. I remember thinking that if he came back, he wouldn't see me walking in the direction he thought I would be walking. I remember the sky becoming dark, and I got lost in the cemetery. I think it was maybe 10-15 minutes past before I saw Dutch riding his bike toward me in the cemetery.

He was riding fast as if he was rushing to find me. I remember me feeling scared and shocked that he still found me and that my plan of trying to throw him off didn't work. As he rode towards me I stood still, thinking to myself, run, but asking myself where am I going to run because I didn't know how to get back out of the cemetery. I remember hiding behind a tombstone and Dutch pulling up to me. The ground felt cold, and I remember feeling very scared. He asked me what I was doing, and I angrily said I can't find my way out of here. He told me he could show me if I wanted him to, and he smiled. I remember thinking he was crazy for thinking I would want any help from him. On the other hand, I felt I didn't have much of a choice if I wanted to make it back home.

I got up from the ground, and he told me to hop on the pegs of his bike so he could ride me out of the cemetery. I did what he said while holding onto the back of shoulders, so I didn't fall. I remember being so angry that I now needed help from someone that had put me through so much pain. I felt very angry and confused. Before finding an exit from the cemetery, he slowed his bike down and told me to hop off. When I asked why we were stopping... he replied I want you to go down on me again before I show you how to get out of here. I remember rolling my eyes and feeling stupid for thinking he would actually help me get out of the cemetery. I remember wondering what kind of weapons he would try to pull out on me if I didn't listen this time. So I just cooperated and did what he asked. After yet another disgusting forceful sexual encounter, he eventually did show me where the exit was and told me to walk home the rest of the way. I remember having to walk over ten blocks to get home that night. I was very upset with myself for being stupid and getting lost.

These events led to my long journey of battling anger problems and major depression. After seven years of persistent suicidal thoughts and not understanding the point of life, I hated every day I woke up from that point on. I tried to talk to my mom about what happened but couldn't find the words to express everything I had gone through. She was always so busy taking care of my father's business and several other children that she didn't have time to listen anyways. My dad worked 20-hour shifts six days per week, so he never was around for me to ask for help. Not that I could share these horrific stories with him anyways. After all, I was daddy's little girl. What would he think of me once he found out his baby girl was damaged goods? I felt very alone and acted out by fighting and pushing people out of my life. Renegade behaviors led to arrests and getting suspended and expelled from good schools. An attempt to overdose on pills didn't work. Therefore, I lived each day, hoping it would be my last.

November 15th, 2008, changed my life. I became a mother to a beautiful baby boy who gave me all the reasons I needed to fight and change my life for good. The first time he was put into my arms after, I looked him in the face and stated, "It's you and me against the world." At that moment, I decided to turn my trials into positive energy that would allow me to protect my son and be a good example for him in life. I graduated high school and received my bachelor's in science from Virginia State University and my master's in clinical social work from Rutgers University. I traveled internationally as a loyal, dedicated, and supportive military spouse while remaining an active and involved parent in my son's life. I'm proud to say I became a Licensed Clinical Social Worker on my 29th birthday and purchased my own home before age 30-years old. I strengthened my relationship with God and gave birth to my second miracle, who gave me a double dose of love and motivation to stay on the right path in my life. I became an advocate and therapist for youth victims of sexual abuse and have been identified as the perpetrator of sex offenses. Years of therapy, prayers, and dedication to being a good mom have got me through many trials. I cannot say I am exactly where I want to be, but I will say I am a long way away from where I started. For this, I am forever grateful.

LETTER TO SELF

Dear Eneri,

You are stronger than you know. I wish you could see your future. You're so beautiful and loved by many. Keep pushing! There is a purpose for your life. It might not feel that way, but it will make sense soon. Your pain will not be in vain. You are so brave. I am so proud of you. You will be so proud of yourself when you reflect on this part of your life. You will be happy to see that you made it through and didn't allow those situations to break you. You may feel like you've lost at times or that others are winning while you're down. But that is the trick of the enemy trying to get you to give up. He knows your worth and how much you are needed on this earth. So he is trying to throw everything at you to make you give up and end your life. KEEP Fighting IRENE! I am here with you. God is here as well. Even if you feel alone, close your eyes and look inside. There is where you will find me cheering you on and God granting you peace. Keep praying! Hang in there. And do not let the problems and people of this world throw you off focus. YOU got This! Fight until got calls you home! Fight back! Keep fighting! Keep Fighting! You are winning! Because you are a CONQUEROR!

Love always,
Your Older Self!

CHAPTER NINE

Butterfly

Deborah Jackson

Well, Trauma Has No Color. The trauma I went through as a child was not a pretty color. My grandparents raised me due to my mother being so young. When she married, I went to live with them at age five. My mother got pregnant with my brother. Jan 1970. In 1971 my stepfather bought my mom a big house in Queens Village, NY. From what I heard; he promised her a house if she gave him a son. He wanted her to focus on caring for their son instead of working. He was an OK stepfather. He was the parent that took us to places like Colony Island Park, Rockaway playland, and shopping in Downtown Brooklyn. He did the best he could to make me feel like I was his daughter

As I got older, my mother and stepfather would fuss and fight a lot. I remember I jumped on him because I was sick of him hitting my mom and calling her names. He broke her jaw, and she couldn't eat. There was so much yelling, cussing, and slamming of the doors. It was hard growing up with a stepfather that beat your mom. I never knew what I was going to come home from school to.

My stepdad was the breadwinner if that is what you want to call it. He told my mom that she did not have to work because he was the man of the house. My mom was not home much. She loved going to BINGO. She didn't like staying home. I would be home with my brother. I remember he used to look for our mother during the nights she stayed out late. When she would stay out late, my stepfather would lock her out and tell me not to let her in. She would come to my window and knock so I could let her in. She slept in my room so he wouldn't fuss. He would come right into my room and tell her to come into their bedroom. She would be drunk and tell him no. I would tell him to get out of my room before I called my grandma. He knew my grandma didn't play when it came to me.

My brother was OK. I always looked after him. I wouldn't let him hurt him. When she washome, she would be with other people. I don't want to put her business out there, but it was crazy; just saying. I am so glad for my grandparents and my aunt. Her sister had a part in making me who I am today. I had to watch my brother to make sure he went to school. The teacher would call me if he did something wrong in school. Growing up in that house was not the best. My mother used to drink and go out and leave me home with my stepfather and two of his nephews. We always had BBQs. My family loved to gamble which often led to everyone playing cards. Our house was big, so my cousins would ask to stay over. Now that I am thinking back, I realize that there was no one there my age.

My brother had his own room. Our cousins would either sleep in his room or the basement. One night they stayed over. That happened to be the same night that my mother and stepfather were drunk. They had no idea what was going on. They went to their room in front of the house. My room was in the back; it was a one-story house. My brother's room was before my room. I went into my room, closed the door, and turned on the television. A few minutes later, I heard someone walking to the bathroom; yes, my room was next to the bathroom. I often remember praying to God that none of them would come into my room. I would be lying there saying, "Please, Please don't let one of them come into my room again". Yes, I said again! It became common for those cousins to find their way into my room when they slept over. It happened often; I just never wanted to relive it.

My cousin would push the door open and say, "Deb" or "Cuz," "are you up"? I hated hearing those words. I wouldn't say anything; I would act like I was asleep. He would climb over me because my bed was close to the wall. I slept on the end of my bed. He would get behind me and move close to my back. He then moved to rubbing on my breast and down my legs. He then turned me over and laid on top of me. I remember closing my eyes. I already knew what would be next. I laid there as he put his penis in my private part. The pain was excruciating. He knew that I was in pain which was why he would say, "I am not hurting you." After he was done, he would get up and tell me that I better not tell anyone, then he went back to my brother's room.

I didn't know what to do so, I cried myself to sleep. I was scared to say anything. I just wanted to go back to my grandmother's house. My grandmother's home was like a place of safety for me. I didn't come out of my room until I heard my brother moving around. I always made sure I was fully dressed before I left my room. The sight of them made my skin crawl. I could not look at them. My stepfather took them home around two in the afternoon. I was so happy. They asked if I could come to their house the following weekend, but I didn't answer them. My stepfather said, "yes, she will not stay here by herself." That weekend I was at my grandparents' house. This went on for some time, and I never told anyone about it. I just knew I hated to see them coming over. My mother never knew; she was clueless about all of the pain I was experiencing right under her nose. All she knew was how to take care of herself.

I had a similar experience while I was in high school. One night my best friend asked me to go with her to see her boyfriend. She didn't like going by herself because the area was dangerous. It would be guys hanging out on the blocks. Girls would go missing and be raped. They would yell out to the girls, "come here." "What are you doing out here this time of night?" It was in Rosedale, the area we had to walk a few blocks to. That's why I didn't want her to go alone. He lived in the apartment building. When we got to his section, we went upstairs to his apartment. His sister was there too. I stayed there for about an hour or two. Then she asked me if I would go across the hall to this guy named "A's" apartment so she could be with her Bo. I really didn't think anything of it. We went to the same high school. I often saw him in school. He was always loud and had to be seen. So, we went over, and they chatted for a minute at the door. I said cool, don't be long. I saw her with A. We sat in the living room. His mother was resting in her bedroom because she had been in a car accident.

He said, "Hey, let's go back to my room and watch television." All the lights were on in his room. We walked to the back past the bathroom and stood by the door. He said, "Deb, come sit on the bed." I sat on the edge of his bed. He left and returned to the room dressed in blue jeans and a T-shirt. Before I knew it, he had thrown me down. He started pulling on my jeans. I was pulling at my pants. I was yelling, "STOP," "STOP," "A," "STOP" His mom yelled, "A," "STOP," get off that girl! He was yelling at her to shut up. He continued pulling on my pants while I was crying and yelling stop. Before I knew it, he had got my pants down enough to put his penis in my private spot. It hurt so bad. I was lying there crying, wondering why this was happening to me.

This man was raping me. He finally got off me, rolled over, and told me to get the Fuck out of his house. I ran out of his room straight to the door. I was crying while I was trying to open the door. I heard him yelling, "YOU BETTER NOT TELL NO ONE," in a voice that scared me. The door opened, and my best friend and her boyfriend were at the door. They say they heard me. Her boyfriend said to "A," "I know you didn't do anything to Deborah." He looked at him like fuck you too. I looked at my friend and said, "Let's go," "I want to go home." His sister asked me if I was OK. I said, "yes." I just wanted to go home. We walked home. I didn't say anything to her on the walk home. She asked me what had happened. I told her nothing in a sad voice.

When I got home, I went straight to the bathroom. My grandma asked me what was wrong. She knew something was wrong because I'd never come home and went straight into the bathroom. I usually go into her room and talk about my crazy best friend. That was the night I didn't have anything to say about her. I took a shower and stayed there for a long time. I stood there crying, wondering why this had just happened to me. I stood there scrubbing my body like it would wash it off, thinking why I should have never gone with my friend. I would never have been raped if I had stayed home.

I got out of the shower and picked up my pants and underclothes, and put them in the trash outside in a bag. I came back upstairs and went to bed. My grandmother asked me again, "Deborah, what is wrong?" I told her my stomach was hurting and I wasn't feeling well. I didn't lie; I didn't feel good about what I had just gone through. I had school the next day, but I did not go. He must have been looking for me at school because he noticed I wasn't there.

He found out where I lived, and I heard knocking on my door. I went running to the door. I opened the door and saw that it was him. He tried to put his foot in the door and asked why I lied. He said, "I didn't RAPE you." I pulled the door and told him to move and get his foot out the way before I called my grandma. He moved his foot, and I closed the door. My grandma asked me who it was, and I told her it was my friend. The school found out he had done something to me. I didn't go to school for about a week. When I returned to school, I was hoping not to run into him. As I was walking in the hallways, I ran into him.

He threw me on the wall and said, "I told you not to say anything." One of my friends walked up and told him to stop and leave me alone. He laughs and walks away like shit was funny.

She walked me to the Guidance office and sat there talking with me. She said, Deb," you should talk to someone." I told her that I would be OK. She said, "if you need me, let me know," I said, "OK." She was the mom of all the girls. She cared a lot about her friends. We are still friends to this day. After this happened, I did not like being around guys by myself. I would think That guys were talking about me to people. I thought he was telling others that I was a hoe. He didn't have the right to rape me; NO, mean NO.

At the age of 13, I moved in with my grandma. I love being at my grandparents' house. I used to live with them when I was born. My mother let my grandma raise me. It was hard for her because she didn't want the man she had sex with, my dad. She didn't want him to be my father. So, she never told him that I was his child. She told her sister, my grandparents, and my aunt not to tell him about me. She also told them not to tell me about him. So, my father just stayed away.

Growing up, she told me this other man was my dad. For years I thought that Mr. F was my dad. He did so much for me as a child. I used to wonder why I didn't look like him or his family. He had a daughter who used to say we don't look alike. I still never looked at that. I thought she just didn't like me. He did so much for me. Do you know what's funny about my birth certificate? She put another man on it! LOL! Not Mr. F, but Mr. W., and none of those Niggers were my dad.

So now you're wondering what happened? My dad stayed away, as she asked. He got married, and he and his wife had twin girls. I was born in June, and they were born in October. He told his wife that he had slept with another woman when he went to New York. He was living in South Carolina at the time. They moved to New York after the twins were born. As time went by, they moved to Hempstead, New York. My Aunt Mae knew he was my dad. She took me to church with her every Sunday, not knowing my dad belonged to the church. He would see me every Sunday and gave my aunt money to give to my grandmother for me. He still never said anything. My sisters would be there too. I had four sisters that I didn't know about. I always had the best of everything. My grandmother made sure of it. Whatever he would give my aunt, she would give to me.

I worked in the mall at a shoe store when I was 17. I remember this man came to the store to buy some wing-toe shoes. They were expensive shoes he wore to church. I brought the shoes out so he could try them on. I went to the back of the store to get another pair for him to try on. When I came back out, he was gone. My boss handed me an envelope and said a man had left it for me. I was confused but decided to open the envelope anyway. There was money in the envelope, but there wasn't a note. I went home to tell my grandma. She asked what he looked like. I told her that he was a tall brown-skinned man. My grandfather made a weird sound like "Sweetie, don't say anything"; she didn't. She said, "Well, maybe he is a family member and gave you a commission for selling the shoes. That same man returned to my job on two other occasions, one with my sister.

Years passed, and I didn't see him again until my grandmother passed away. My grandma was buried in Clark Hill, South Carolina. It was summertime, and my dad was down there visiting his mom and family in Clark Hill too. (Pay attention) We were at my uncle's house having the repass dinner. I had three children of my own at that time. All my family was at the dinner, my grandfather, aunt, uncle, and other family members. My mom was inside the house. My son was only seven months, so she was watching him. I came outside, and everyone was talking to each other. It was funny how he just happened to be at a repass dinner. My grandfather was sitting in the van, and he opened the door while smoking a cigarette. My aunt, mother, sister, husband, and Aunt Mae (the one that took me to church) were there. Then this man was standing there talking.

I get up to talk to my aunt, and he comes out and says, "DO YOU KNOW WHO I AM"? I reply, "No," with what the HELL! Face. He said, "I am your DAD!!" I looked over at my grandfather, and he shook his head. YES. I looked at my aunt, and she said, "YES." I was in shock. I couldn't believe it. I ran into my uncle's house and yelled at my mother. I saw some man with them who said I am your dad. She was pissed. She started cussing, saying, "HG better not be out telling people that." She goes to the door, and he is right there. My grandfather said she needed to know. She told all of them to kiss her where the sun didn't shine (laughing at this part). I went outside and finished talking to my grandfather while he was getting his story together. We talked for a minute.

I didn't know what to say, he gave me his number and told me to call him. We left that Sunday night to head back to New York. That car ride was so silent that you could hear a pin drop. My mother didn't talk to anyone for fourteen hours. I didn't speak to her for about two weeks when I returned home. I didn't have anything to say. I let weeks go by. I didn't know what to say. Did I have sisters? Did his wife know about me? All types of things were running through my head. I called him, and he asked me where I lived. I told him that I lived in Bricktown,

Jamaica, Queens. I gave him the address, and he came by in this big, long-island railroad truck.

All that time, my father worked right around the corner from my home. When I say around the corner from my house, I can walk to his job. The visit was nice. It was like I knew him. He made me feel like he had been waiting for that moment. My mom was mad that I had talked to him. She asked me not to say his name around her. I feel in my heart my grandma sent him to watch over me and her grandkids. What he did was so real. I had four sisters. I look like my older sister, and we are all built the same. We all work with children. It's crazy. The only thing I don't like is I didn't grow up with them, but we all love each other the same. His wife is the best bonus mom a girl can have. She took me in with no problem. I am so grateful for everything he has done for me. He passed away last year. He will always be in my heart. My bonus mom and sisters are all very close as of today.

After the sexual abuse and rape, life was different for me when it came to guys. I didn't want to be around guys. I developed very quickly. I had breasts in the fourth grade. I remember boys would try to run up to me and grab them. I would be so mad I would tell them to stop. I would go home and tell my mom. She wouldn't say much. As I got older, I felt uncountable being around guys because I would feel like they were looking at my breast. When I did get into a relationship with a guy, I would be scared if they wanted to have sex. I wondered if they would take NO for an answer or try to take it like it had been taken in my past. I would have sex with guys thinking that's what I was supposed to do. Life was so confusing. Because I was raped, it was hard for me to know what men wanted me for. I wouldn't rush to have sex with no guys, and I would never again allow myself to be in a place where something could happen. I didn't sleep with my husband for three months, and when I did, I cried. I thought he would leave me because I gave it up.

Despite my trauma, I was still able to have healthy relationships. I met a guy, and we talked about my life. He knew everything I had been through. We got married, and unfortunately, he went to prison, not knowing he would be in the same prison where my rapist was. One day, he was chatting it up with him, walking to his cell. He went into his cell and saw my picture on my husband's cell wall. He looked at the picture and asked my husband if he knew who I was. My husband said, "Why"! He said, "I got that!" My ex-husband said, "WHAT THE HELL IS YOUR NAME!!!" He said "A," and my husband beat his ASS and gave him two black eyes.

That same weekend I went to visit my husband in prison. He sat down and hugged me. He was supposed to be put in the box for fighting. "A" came out next. When I saw his face, he had two black eyes. He couldn't even walk well. He was hurt. My husband gave him a real ASS BEATING. I can say, "Laugh Now," "Who HAD The Laugh"; Me. Justice was served. But I still have to live with it. I didn't stay married to my husband for long, and I remarried after I got divorced.

I'm happy to say that it's 28 years later, and we have six kids, of which two are married, and nine grandkids. We are still together. I was so hard on my children. I was very overprotective. I always talked to them about going out and being around their guy friends. I didn't let them stay in places where I knew there would be boys around. In my head, all men couldn't be trusted around my girls. Now that I have a counselor, I was able to understand why I was like that toward my girls. Sometimes I still think about what if I had talked about this earlier in life, things for me would have gone differently. My kids were often upset with me because I restricted them from doing a lot of stuff. All of my children are grown, even my baby daughter. I still call her to make sure she is OK. It still will take time to feel whole. I feel like I got it together, but now I have a grandkid that I think about. I've always told them to tell someone if anyone touches them inappropriately. My eyes will never be closed to rape. It is just easy to talk to people that might need advice.

LETTER TO SELF

Dear Deborah,

You had to learn the hard way. Being molested young and raped made you scared to tell anyone. You had to keep this a secret for all these years. Not feeling wealthy. Not feeling love As time passes, you will learn not to be scared of no one. I Am sorry you had so much pain in your life. I am sorry you had to see your mom get beat by her husband. I am sorry you had to wait to meet your dad when your grandma passed. I am sorry you let men do things to you because you didn't know better. You will learn not to let people do what they want to you. You will be strong. You are wealthy.

Whatever you decide to be, be the best at it. Don't let people make you feel you're not worthy or that there's anything you can't do. Never be scared to let someone know you have been touched in the wrong place on your body by a man. Don't be scared to be yourself. Whatever you want to be in life, be the best you can be. Don't let NO ONE say that you can't be a Doctor, Nurse, Lawyer, or writer. Be a leader, not a follower; love yourself. Always put yourself first. You will be surprised how your life will turn out. Your life would be so great. You may have some ups and downs but get back on the road, put a smile on that face, hold your head up, and say the devil is a lie. YOU GOT THIS!!

CHAPTER TEN

The Tone Of Resilience

Devaron Flint

Trauma has allowed me to create several masks in order to push through. The problem with wearing so many masks for so long is that they somehow become a part of you. I do not like to think of these "masks" or experiences as positive or negative, as they had served me in moments when they were needed. A common theme for my masks has been control. As a child, I often felt control less. Things happened in my life that often left me feeling voiceless and powerless. I do not recall when I made myself the promise, but I recall telling myself at some point, I would be in the driver's seat and never give that spot up again. That promise of this illusion of control has given me balance. I also feel like the idea of needing control was shown to me by my mother, who learned it from my grandmother. They both experienced horrible things that happened to them, such as sexual assault, poverty, addiction, and domestic violence.

I believe a way to escape the heaviness of it all; they created this idea of control and resilience. That no matter what happened, they could push through it. This has been my mantra. When I think about my strengths, it is the first thing that comes to mind. My experiences have seemed to only intensify my strengths as where I was once someone who felt voiceless, I now advocate for myself, my loved ones, and anyone who I happen to cross paths with. I am empathetic as I often had to read the room growing up quickly due to my mother's addiction to crack cocaine.

My mother had grown up in an impoverished environment. However, she was taught by her mother always to make sure no one outside of her home knew what she was going through, as that was a private matter. When you stepped outside, the way you looked and presented yourself would be instantly judged. My mother mastered this concept, so every time we left our home everything was in order, from the hair barrette to the matching family outfits. Although community gossip still took place, the picture, for the most part, never seemed to match those discussions. This idea helped my creativity grow as well, as when you have limited resources but are still asked to meet or exceed the mark, you learn to adapt quickly and figure out how to use what you have to create what you need or want. Those lessons made me driven, determined and shaped a go-getter attitude within me.

I refused to be treated as less than, viewed as a victim, or, God forbid, people feel sorry for me. My mother also ensured that we knew no matter how bad we thought, we had something that someone else was praying to have what we did, and so we had to always give back in some manner. Due to this, I am continuously giving to others, whether it be with my time, gifts, donations, or services.

LEAVES

I often view my traumatic experiences as if they are live films set in a view master that I can decide when to click through. This, again, goes back to my need for control. I like to look at them from the viewpoint of things that I experienced that have molded me into the person I am today. The roots of my trauma have strengthened the foundation of my being as they give so much context to understanding me. My relationship with faith and believing in something much bigger than you is rooted in my experiences with my mom's addiction to crack cocaine. Me and my sisters experienced several things due to her addiction, and without believing in something greater, I am not sure I would have been able to get through it all.

Another key root is order and determination. While these roots were created to try and cope with chaos, they assisted in being building blocks for whenever I faced adversity or challenge. When I knew I wanted to pursue higher education, I didn't have any real guidance, access to important documents to register, funding, or strong transcripts. I relied heavily on these to continue pushing forward regardless of my barriers. My loyalty is also an area I am thankful for. Not loyalty in the sense of blindly being there for someone but loyalty where I will give you support and be there on your darkest and brightest days. I will give you feedback, encouragement, and support to help you meet your goals. I will remind you of your potential even when it is not clear to you. My belief in my mother kept me as a touchstone to her even when she no longer believed in herself. I would be honest with her when she needed it, but I always told her I was willing to get in the arena with her if needed. I continued to stand with a guiding light like a lighthouse even when she seemed to be surrounded by complete darkness in hopes that she would eventually see the light and make her way toward me.

That loyalty allowed me to see my mother clean from her addiction and be a better caregiver to her grandchildren than she had been to her children. I continuously reminded my mother of who she was fully, both the good and the bad; even with it all, she still deserved love, support, time, understanding, and growth. My loyalty over time has developed better boundaries; however, it allows me to meet people where they are, love them, and support them in some manner that I think everyone needs.

When I reflect on how I got through some of the challenges in my life, I instantly think about key people who made a significant difference in my life. My grandmother and her boyfriend, who we always called our grandfather, took us school shopping, allowed us to have birthday parties at their homes, took us on trips, and just tried to give us great memories growing up even in the midst of chaos. My aunt and uncle took us into their home numerous times when my mom was actively struggling with her addiction, even though they were younger and had their own family to raise. My uncle never made us feel as if we were different or not family, even though he was only connected to us from marriage. That made such a huge difference to me as he did not have to step up, but he chose to. Finally, my godmother gave me structure and support. She would get onto me about school work but was also willing to take the time and make sure I had what I needed to succeed and exceed the standard. She has been a cheerleader of all my accomplishments, continuously encouraging me to be better than I was.

My bonus mom continuously worked at tearing down the walls I put up and ensured that I knew that love was an action, not just a word. She taught me that no matter how you start off, anything is possible if you put in the work. She also taught me that you could build your tribe if the one you were born into is not fulfilling the job. Another powerful lesson she taught me was understanding, forgiveness, limitless love, and creating a foundation. No matter where I go or what barriers I face, I know that I always have someone in my corner and a place to call home, which has given me such freedom and peace of mind. She gets me in ways that many will never be able to. She is my person who keeps me balanced and inline no matter what course my life takes.

My husband is another person who has strongly impacted my life as he was something I was not looking for and did not know I needed. He is a constant in a world I had learned was unstable. He listens to my dreams and supports my goals. He gives me balance while also giving me space to heal from my challenges. He also allowed me space to assist my mom, sisters and their children, allowing me to do necessary healing and demolish generational curses. He also has shown me that men like my uncle are not unicorns and will step up and give unwavering support to those they love. Loving my mother and sisters even when they are not at their best.

My relationship with my parents has had highs and lows as they both had their own personal struggles that impacted who they were as parents. However, it is because of those personal struggles that they have taught me a lot. Both my parents faced significant hardships as children dealing with situations no child should experience, and yet they gave love a chance and came together, allowing me and my sisters to be born. They both craved love and desired to build their own family unit as they felt their families had failed them in many ways. The idea was good; however, their execution was not. They were two young adults who were trying to love each other while still discovering who they were and attempting to heal wounds that never seemed to stay close. They had very strong ideas on how they believed their partners and their family should be, and unbeknown to them, those ideas were molded by their parents, whom they were trying to escape. My parents taught me that you do not have to accept life as you have known it to be and that change is possible if you are willing to put in the work.

My father taught me how to dream big and work hard. My mother taught me to look for the good in people, lead with a generous spirit, heart, and grit, never accept the word no, and always bet on yourself. My father taught me the importance of second chances; growing up he was not as present as he or I would have liked due to things bigger than us. I initially resented him for this; however, after I graduated from high school and relocated to Florida, we were able to grow our relationship and see each other through a different lens. This led to my understanding of the importance of acceptance, opportunities for forgiveness, and how our experiences create a lens that impacts how we view the world.

DEPENDENCE

She came home again and was met with the routine of a warm bath with Epson salt run by my grandmother. Hair and clothes were washed after the pockets were disposed of. I was very familiar with this routine. I knew she wouldn't want anything to eat and that the next few days would be the hardest for her. She made it home, and that is what I chose to focus on, but I still was left with so many different feelings and unable to discuss them with the very person responsible for them. I had faked sick that day to stay home from school in hopes that she would come home and find someone waiting for her. I was mad at her for leaving and staying away for so long. I was also relieved that she had returned. After she got into bed and slept for a few hours, I sneaked into the room just to make sure she knew I had waited for her. I climbed into the bed and asked if I could lay with her. She was awake and restless but pulled me closer and wrapped her arms around me. I told her I knew she would come back and hoped she would stay this time. That I loved her, and my sisters would be excited to see her when they came home from school.

We lay in silence while she just held onto me; however, her grasp seemed to get tighter at one point, and her face, which was lying close to mine, started to feel wet. She started crying harder and holding me tighter and tighter. She told me that she was sorry she just could not get it right and that she loved my sisters and me so much and wanted to be there for us; however, she was sick. At that time, I knew my mom had struggled with drugs and that they were a bad thing however did not have a real understanding of the hold they could have on people. I asked my mom why her love for us did not make her get better and why she kept doing something that made her so sad and sick. I did not realize the weight of the question at the time, as my mom never gave me an answer. She kept repeating that she was trying, fighting and that she knew she did not deserve our forgiveness or love but loved us more than herself and to never forget that. I repeated a simple "I know" and then we sat there in silence.

My grandmother came and got me from the room to let my mom rest for a while. While downstairs, I asked my grandmother if my mom was better now, and she said that she was trying to be and that she just needed some time away to become a better mom to us. I knew that this meant she was going away to another rehab. I did not understand why it was so hard for her or why she had to leave to become better when all my friends had moms who never seemed to have to leave. My aunt had three children, and she never needed to leave. My grandmother, who raised my mom, aunt, and uncle, was again helping to raise us and never left. I also could not understand how we were continuously told my mom needed time to become a better mom; however, every time she came back, the new version seemed to only be made for demonstration because the periods always had time limits. My sisters and I tried to be on our best behavior to make it easier to be our mom, but that still wasn't enough to keep her there.

We never knew what would cause her to get upset or when she would run off, just that we would be left once again abandoned trying to come up with answers as if we were given a jigsaw puzzle to solve with pieces missing and unsure what the completed picture should look like. I knew that my mom could be a good mom as she was a lot of fun, thoughtful, caring, selfless, giving, funny, protective, and loving at times. However, she also could be mean, irritable, hurtful, disconnected, immature, and impulsive. It was like living with a real-life Jekyll and Mr. Hyde. Never knowing who you would be dealing with at any moment but knowing that both made up the person you loved. The conflict inside my mother seemed to also create a conflict inside of myself. On my hand, I resented her for not being strong enough to choose herself or us; on the other hand, I felt empathy for her as I knew she had been through so much and yet continued to fight and try. I, at times, thought her to be both weak and strong. Both a person of redemption as well as just simply surviving. A mother as well as just a person who gave me life. A person who at times nurtured me and other times was the one who required to be nurtured.

TRUST

Finally, I made it to the sweet 16 milestone and had only a few more years until I could fully be in the driver's seat of my own life. I got a call to hang out with some friends for the evening, so I invited my two sisters, who are always down for a good time. Plus, taking my older sister will allow my grandma to give us a later curfew. We arrived on the scene, and there were some girls we did not know but seemed to want to have a good time. Card game with music loudly playing in the background in the basement. I was excited to be hanging with the group as I grew up around the guys who lived in the house and always had a crush on the younger one. Drinks were offered, starting with beer, then cups of liquor poured and offered. The smell of newports and black and milds filled the air. "I wonder if he likes me?" I thought.

I was not like the other girls he seemed to be into prior. Some laughs were shared completely clueless about the card game but watching, making comments, and laughing. As time continued, the drinks all began to taste the same but never stopped coming. The room started to spin, but I could not figure out if it was from the smoke smell impacting my eyes or the alcohol finally hitting the pasta I had eaten earlier in the night not agreeing. A familiar kind smile offering to help me find somewhere quiet to rest found me and seemed to help the room slow down in its spinning. I attempted to stand but was met with my legs not fully being able to hold or carry me. I was stumbling with the support of two of the guys assisting me. I cannot believe I had gotten like this as I had always been known to be a heavy drinker with a high tolerance. Take it step by step. I overhear a familiar voice in the background, "She going to be okay," and that "she seems messed up." Again encouraged to continue up the steps as my younger sister had been taken to the same place due to not feeling well too. A sense of comfort came over me. I was so glad that even though I had been feeling the alcohol more than I would like, I was surrounded by people I knew and trusted. Again reassuring me that I was in good hands and referred to me as 'sis'.

After every few steps, my body seemed to yell out warnings not to continue with gut-wrecking discomfort, which would end with vomit, and my eyes felt so heavy that it took so much energy to keep them open. I continued to apologize for the evidence I continued to leave throughout my journey in their house to a quiet place where I was supposed to rest at. My eyes felt even heavier, and rest seemed to be calling my name. I lay in bed and was reassured that I was good and there were no hurt feelings about the mess I had made while in transit. At ease, I allowed my eyes to close. Rest was the only antidote to the room spinning, and I happily accepted it.

Hands touching my shirt. Cold lips felt on my neck met at my ear, whispering, "everything is okay." My body no longer feels like my own. The buttons on my pants no longer feel secure. What is happening? Did I ask for this? Did I say it was okay? Did I say no? This was not how it was supposed to happen. What would people say? Why had I allowed myself to be in this situation? Eyes were again getting heavy. Not yet I need to speak up. I was fighting against myself and losing the battle. Again, awoken to my pants gone and arguing in the background. "What are you doing"? Are you dumb? "Get out of here." Finally, someone spoke up and said the words that would not escape my lips. He attempted to put my underwear and pants back on. Finally, someone who was protective and thoughtful.

Eyes getting heavy again. I was able to mouth the words thanks, or at least in my head. I verbally said the words. Eyes again were getting heavy; however, this time, I felt safe, so I allowed it. Warm breath in my ear and pain from in between my legs. The person I thought was my savior turned out to be a wolf in sheep's clothing. He was not protecting me but wanting me to himself. My body was no longer my own. One...two...three...four pumps when I saw a shadow come and snatch him off me. And just like that, I was just like my mom and grandmother, our bodies no longer our own and violated not by strangers but those we knew and trusted. When I got home, I hurried to the shower and tried to wash the night's mistakes away. As the water washed over me, I let my tears flow so the shower could disguise my sorrow. I had told myself so many times that I would never be like my mother, but at this moment, she was probably one of the few people who knew how I truly felt, and still, I never said a word.

SECURITY

Junior year —

I was over feeling like the maid and babysitter and like nothing I did was enough to live here. I packed my clothes in a duffle bag and put it in the second-floor bedroom. My plan was to come back from play practice and leave while everyone was sleeping. After I was dropped off at the house, my plan began to take form. I walked up the steps to the second floor and considered going into the attic to get additional items to take with me; however, before I could touch the door handle, a creepy feeling overcame my body warning me to not go into my room. I had a fear of the dark and hated going into the attic as depending on how the last person turned off the switch; you could either turn the light on at the bottom of the stairs or you had to climb all the stairs in darkness until you reached the second switch that was in the middle of the room.

That uneasy feeling was like nothing I had ever felt before, and I decided to listen to my body. I went into the bedroom where my cousin slept and got some clothes out to take a shower. I had no real idea where I was heading, but I knew tonight would be the night for me to leave. I took a shower and then got on the phone with one of my best friends to see how I could make my exit. I was laughing and chatting when I overheard my name being yelled from the back bedroom. Ugh, here it goes. I agreed to be quiet, apologize, and continue talking with my friend. Again, I heard my name being called from the back bedroom, some other words that I could not distinguish. I walked into her office, which connects to their bedroom, to make out what she was saying better. "Stop talking so loud. Everyone is sleeping, and the twins are in the front bedroom, and I don't want them up".

Annoyed once again, I'm the problem. I apologized and began walking out of her office when I saw bright red flames from the window. Surprised, shocked, and intrigued, I walk to the window. Yell out, the neighbor's house is on fire". My aunt comes out of her bedroom still fussing at me for being so loud. I again say out loud, "the neighbor's house is on fire." "No, wait, it's our house that is on fire." The words continued to come from my mouth, getting louder and louder with panic; however, my body seemed at first unable to move. Then instantly, I began running through the second floor of our house, yelling and getting everyone up and out of our home that was on fire.

We struggled at first to get into one of the bedrooms where my cousin and two of our younger cousins were sleeping. The twins were toddlers at the age where they would open doors and get into mischief, so a toybox was put in front of the door to keep them inside. We also could not initially locate my younger cousin as he had decided to sleep in his mother's room for the night so that his room could be used to house the twins and his older sister. Panic continued to fill our home while we attempted to ensure everyone made it out safely. Once outside, I remembered our dog was still in my uncle's man cave in the back room on the first level and ran back in to get her.

When we came back outside, the fire trucks had finally arrived, and all our neighbors had formed in the streets. We all just watched as the firefighters attempted to save our home. A home that I had made plans to leave but now prayed for another night in. I watched as the fire blazed through the attic where my cousin and I slept. I thought about how close I was to opening the door to that attic. We stood there in the cold with tears in our eyes as we watched our home burn with all our personal items gone with it. I had grown used to losing personal items due to my mom's addiction, but this was new. This was a home in which I felt safe and secure for a while, and now it had left me. My aunt told us that we would get through this as we stood outside the burning house; however, little did I know that her words had different meanings for me verse her actual family unit. They would be separated living with the homes of my uncle' parents and her mother's house until they found their new home and I would be living between the homes of my friends going into my senior year.

VULNERABILITY

It finally happened; the day I had worked so hard for had arrived. My sister took me to get my hair and nails done. My sisters and mom had our times to arrive at the school, and my out-of-town family had gotten in safely. I was overjoyed as soon I would be heading to Florida to live with my older cousin and starting off my new chapter, where I made the calls. I called my best friends to discuss our outfits, iron out the pick-up time they would be arriving to head to the school, and attempt to finalize our later evening plans. Excitement can be heard from down the hall. His back pay money had come in.

It had been a memorable night. A night that we all would remember as we soon would enter the next chapter of our lives with some going off to college, relocating to new places, or beginning full-time jobs with real responsibilities. Friends had fallen asleep wherever they finally crashed after the evening events throughout the house. Suddenly a loud voice is heard coming through the kitchen. "Get up and get out." The voice, loud and angry, sounded familiar; however, I could not place it. What is going on? "Get up and get the fuck out." "Y'all are being evicted." "Your mom is months behind on her rent, and she was supposed to be paying what was due yesterday and never showed." The angry voice was getting closer to my resting spot. Finally, the voice and face are able to be made out. My mom's best friend and landlord. There has to be a mistake. "Don't touch shit, and everyone get out." My older sister tried to get answers that were only met with more anger. Trying to minimize what my friends are hearing, I attempt to reassure her this is a simple misunderstanding, but she is not listening to my reasoning. She continues to yell about my mom, her addiction mixed with profanities. My graduation party and shoes are upstairs. My older sister attempted to reach my mom with no success. No one was supposed to know about this part of my life. I felt like I was in the middle of a packed mall with a person reading my deepest and darkest secrets over the intercom. Why was my mom not answering? They just got that sum of money in, so why didn't they pay the back due money?

My older sister took over, trying to grab whatever items she could in her hands to take to her car. My friend comes back inside and says, "mmm, your sister's car is not here." And just like that, all the warning signs leading up to this moment start replaying rapidly before my eyes. My mom never made it to the restaurant to celebrate my graduation. She was supposed to come but then texted saying she was going to be late. Then as time went on, she texted saying she was not going to make it at all. She was beyond happy to offer to stay in a hotel for the evening, even saying my sisters and I could have the house for the night. My mom never parented us like a hawk. However, she was also not into giving teenagers free rein unless she wanted free range. The hotel, limited communication, back due rent, and now my sister's car is missing. How could I not see this? It happens like this every time. She comes back, makes her promises, tries her hardest to get life back on track, and just when we finally let our guard down, that monkey on her back always wins the fight.

She came in town with a check that could have helped take care of our house and even given me a nice start on my new chapter in Florida but instead, the cycle continued. My older sister came back into the house, and the look on her face was a mixture of anger, defeat, loss, and returned pain. I could tell she was trying to put on a brave face for us, especially as we were not alone in facing this reality. We now had an audience who were witnesses to this tragic cycle. My friends were all trying to be helpful and not address the elephant in the room. They just kept asking what or how they could help. My sisters and I had been through this so many times; however, each time never seemed to get easier. I kept repeating to myself, "I cannot wait to be out of this place." "She is dead to me."

Our landlord was still yelling and fussing in the background; however, I had tuned her out at this point. I knew what was going on and had to numb myself again. I could not allow this to stop me from doing what I knew needed to be done. I could no longer continue to try to save my mom, as saving her often meant slowly killing myself. I had always believed my love for her was enough to save her, even if that meant putting myself at risk. We would go through the cycle of her using, leaving for hours, days, weeks, and sometimes months. I would convince myself that as long as I stayed, she would always come back because she would know someone was waiting who loved her unconditionally. I stayed even when others called child services on her, and they would attempt to interview us at school. I stayed even when she smoked up all the food stamps and we had nothing to eat in the house. I stayed even when she used up all the funds, so the utilities got turned off leaving us to have to heat the house with the oven or boil water to take bathe with. I stayed even when the houses we lived in should have been condemned. I stayed even when personal items went missing, we lost family pets and important belongings lost due to being evicted. I stayed even when I should have been in school, caring about making good grades or just being a child. While my friends were enjoying their weekends, I traveled to rehab centers for family day. I stayed through all the different jobs, locations, boyfriends, and new beginnings that always were promised to be a new chapter. I continuously stayed because I thought my love for her was enough. However, finally, at age 17, I learned the entire time I was staying, I never paid attention to my roommate, who had been there the entire time, which was her addiction.

My friends helped us pack up the small amount of belongings our landlord allowed us to take in their cars and took us to our aunt's house. Who was getting things ready for my graduation party. One of my best friends took my sister to different known crack houses to try and locate my mom and get her car. My sister ended up seeing her car and attempted to enter to get her keys and my mom. My mom never confirmed she was there or said a word to my sister, but my sister's keys appeared outside the door. To this day, my friend will not mention anything from that day unless I bring it up. She was an 18-year-old who saw some of my ugliest truths and has never wavered. She and my other friend simply asked what was needed and got right to work. We had been good friends prior to this, but it was at that moment that I knew they were my tribe. There was no real discussion, just a look and then action. I never felt so exposed yet also understood. The support they showed me that day allowed me to stop feeling shame for things that were outside of my control.

My aunt had already been given the news and was trying to keep her emotions together as there was a party she was now fully responsible for. My mom had saved up her some of her food stamps that were supposed to cover the food; however, it would be delusional to think this was still an option. My aunt informed me that I would need to call my father to see what he could do as she could not cover the food. I knew my dad would be elated to hear yet another story of my mother crashing out and take this opportunity to tell me how worthless she and her family were. I also knew that I had already dealt with enough embarrassment and that my celebration would be canceled if I did not figure something out to cover the food. I called my father and listened to him give me an ear full about my mother and her side of the family and all the ways they wronged him and then finally had him speak to my aunt, where he agreed to send funds to cover the food. As relieved as I was to still be having my celebration, this exchange reminded me of how I was tolerated for many parts of my life.

I called my older cousin and told her I was ready to just leave this place as soon as my graduation party was over. She purchased me a ticket, and I made my arrangements to get to the airport. I boarded a plane to Florida with pretty much the clothes on my back, no personal documents such as an id, birth certificate, social security card, or even a cell phone. I also boarded the plane without saying goodbye to my mom. She had stopped by towards the end of my graduation party, looking defeated and accepting the crumbs of empathy given to her by our family and loved ones, but I had no real words for her. I was done with trying to understand her and be there unlimited. I hated her for what she had put me through and how many times she chose her addiction over us, and even during one of the most memorable times of my life, her addiction took center stage.

CHANGE OF PLANS

I had always told myself that if I did not wish for something, it would not hurt when it never happened. I had convinced myself that I was fully content without you or that I had no desire for what you had to offer but I soon learned I had been fooling myself. I got to experience what it would be like to have you, and it opened up feelings I never knew I could feel for something like you. Before those experiences, I had been guarded with my love, only giving space to a select few who had proved to be safe. However, once I had those experiences, a part of me yearned for you. I decided it was safe enough to pursue you and began planning how to make it happen. I initially started off with lines in the sand. I think it made me feel more in control and safe; however, I quickly learned that those lines could be washed away quickly and were not permanent. Before I knew it, I was fully invested and willing to do anything for the chance with you. I stabbed myself in the stomach several times in pursuit of you. I allowed strangers to run painful tests and took multiple samples for you. I also used most of my vacation and sick days and ran up my credit card, pursuing you. I changed my lifestyle in hopes for you. I changed my goals and dreams for you.

We had decided to take a break from fertility treatments after our first success ended in a loss at six weeks. My body did not want to let go of the pregnancy, although the baby was no more, so after waiting a few weeks, our doctor provided medication to help me pass what was remaining. It was one of the hardest things I ever had to do in the privacy of my own home. The physical and emotional pain was enough for me to no longer consider moving forward with starting a family. Then a trip to the emergency room for a random issue resulted in me learning not only was I pregnant again, but there was a strong heartbeat. Sitting in the hospital room, I listened to one of my favorite tunes, and tears slowly came down my face.

A rainbow baby I was not expecting had come in full force, making its presence known. As soon as I left the hospital, I researched everything I could about my current journey, the best OBGYNs in the area that my insurance covered, and what

I could do to ensure I kept the pregnancy. My body began changing, and I felt a sense of comfort with every new changing thing. We waited impatiently for our 10-week ultrasound and smiled the entire time while awaiting for the technician to enter the room. The technician was a younger female who was excited and congratulated us on our rainbow baby as she had read over our paperwork before entering the room. She talked us through how the ultrasound would go and that maybe we could have some better pictures of our baby during the visit as I was further along than before.

I was both excited and nervous as we had initially promised ourselves that we would not allow ourselves to get too excited until after the first 12 weeks; however, I instantly forgot that promise soon as I made it. I had already thought about names, what qualities our child would have, the gender, and the different memories I intended to make with them. I thought about who they would become and how we would spend their first birthday. Who they would like better, myself or my spouse, and who would be more wrapped around their finger. The girl started off trying to do the ultrasound via my stomach as I should have been far enough for this. She kept putting more cold gel on my stomach and repositioning the device.

She was no longer as talkative as before, and her excitement started to wear down. As she continued to move around the device on my stomach, I asked if everything was okay. She quickly responded by asking me how far along I was and when was my last period. I explained to her what the doctor at the hospital said and that my periods were irregular, so I was unsure of the date. She then said that sometimes babies were stubborn and that a vaginal ultrasound could be more helpful. Instantly I started to get knots in my stomach but continued to put on a brave face for my spouse. She began the vaginal ultrasound again, continuing to reposition the device, and now she had gone mostly silent, and her responses to our questions were even more textbook. The doctor will review your ultrasound and speak with you shortly were the words she quickly told us as I was directed to get dressed.

My spouse and I shared a few words with each other, thinking about the possibilities that could cause us to speak only with the doctor. The doctor quickly enters the room and says, "there is no heartbeat detected, and the size of the fetus does not reflect where it should be, " which further tells us that the fetus stopped growing and the pregnancy is no longer viable". He gave us some of the worst news we would ever receive with a straight face and cold tone. His next words were that his reports would be sent to our doctor, who will discuss the next steps. We walked out of the office, and logically we knew we had lost another baby, but hope continued to creep in. I still felt pregnant.

The dreams I had just thought of were still vivid in my head, replaying over and over again on repeat. This was our rainbow baby; there was no way they would come into our lives so loudly and then leave out so silently. I was not ready for this to be the end, so I researched ultrasound mistakes and stories about people being told certain things by doctors when pregnant who later ended up giving birth to a healthy baby. I made myself believe that all the feelings I was having physically and emotionally were our baby fighting to be given a chance.

My OBGYN got us in at their office within a few days after our ultrasound visit, and even as I walked through the doors, had made myself believe that the news would be positive. I was going to be told that our baby was just being stubborn, that a heartbeat had been detected, and that I would be meeting them within a few months. The doctor and I were not on the same page in our thinking. She met me with empathy and attempted to provide comforting words as she informed me that all the dreams I had regarding this baby would be no more. I still felt pregnant, not because our baby was alive but because my body was once again refusing to accept the loss. My levels were starting to decline but not fast enough, and the doctor feared the impact this could have on me medically should she not perform a procedure. I felt completely numb. I walked into the office and sat in a waiting room with women at different stages of their pregnancy journeys while mine was over before it even truly began.

SHATTERING

It all began with an unanswered call. The day started off just as any other day. The kids are sleeping in late in their bedroom downstairs. My husband is in his office working. It was a little after 11 am. Sitting in the living room on the sofa when I heard my phone ding. The notification said Ma. I opened my texts to see the message "I can't." I quickly began to text back, "huh," but before I could hit send, another text came in "She's gone." My heart dropped, and the air in the room seemed thicker, making each breath harder to take instantly. My calls continued to go unanswered. My fingers seemed to be delayed in typing; however, I finally got out the words 'who.' Time seemed to stop, and the world around me seemed to pause for a moment. The text message displayed moving dots indicating a message was coming however that message seemed to be coming via horseback as it seemed forever before I saw the response.

Two simple letters caused my entire life to rapidly replay via a snapshot in front of my eyes. All the memories, promises, experiences, and plans are finalized instantly. All the what–ifs no longer have endless possibilities. The person I had finally come to fully understand and had just begun creating a new chapter which seemed to have promise of being the best yet no longer had the ability for a new book volume to be written. The person who was my first love, first heartbreak, first experience of pain, first experience of true resilience, redemption, true forgiveness, teacher of unconditional support was no longer able to be my lifetime teacher. The two letters seemed to be carried by a train that collided directly into my heart and broke it into a million pieces. My entire footing left me, and my body was suddenly free falling with no end in sight, surrounded by nothing as if I were in a dark hole, reaching out and grabbing nothing in hopes of stopping or preventing the fall.

The text read, "Ma."

Followed by back-to-back texts from my mother's phone that read:

"She is gone"

"Her body is blue."

"I can't."

And then silence. No response to my continued texts or calls.

I felt as if my body was just going through the motions of continuously trying to get answers while my mind regressed back to a small girl sitting silently in a corner with so many thoughts, scared of what would happen next. I tried to scream out multiple times, but the feeling of being voiceless came back with a vengeance. I would open my mouth, and no sound would come out. I could not escape. I was trapped, and everything around me was no longer within reach. The tears came easily but did nothing to ease the pain. I had felt loss before, but this loss was soul-wrenching. All the different stages of grief hit me, like being in a fun house room at a carnival with distorted mirrors and flashing lights. Tricking me into trying to make sense of these texts and information. How did this happen? Why did my sister have her phone? Who was responsible? Did all the stress from dealing with my sisters and trying to raise their children finally get to her? Who was going to take care of everyone? Who was going to take care of me? Why did she make it through 24-plus years of crack addiction to have it all end like this? Our relationship was untypical to many as oftentimes I was in the mother role and she in the child role, but we were actively working on changing this. How cruel this joke was to make me believe she had left me indefinitely like that. She had left me in the past, but she always returned. Why would this time be any different? Thousands of questions and thoughts continuously surrounded me.

Then came the text message that read, 'EMT workers had arrived and were performing CPR. Hope proudly arrived, and although I knew with our rocky relationship not to become grounded in her, I still falsely allowed myself to find comfort again in her promise. The future promises started to resume reminding me that our story was not over. We had overcome so much together. What could we not face and get through? This was just another chapter in our story, and we will have yet another chapter filled with trauma and redemption. I said our prayer, the one I had created when I was a child that demanded that God again cover and protect my mom as she had so much more to do and was so much more than what she had been and that she was needed.

Again I tried calling her phone back to back, and my calls continued to go unanswered. Thoughts began to consume me again, and I felt myself beginning to fall again. Please, this cannot be true. This cannot be the end. How do I get through this? How can I get my sisters through this? How do the grandchildren recover from this? I am not strong enough to take this loss on. This cannot be my reality. A call to my aunt was met with no answer. A call to my oldest cousin also went unanswered. Feelings of helplessness are increasing. My body continues to free fall with every attempt to connect with something or someone being met with unsuccess. A text saying, 'please call me; it's an emergency. Sent to follow my unanswered call to my older cousin. My cousin called me and was met with panic while I informed her of the chaos I had been trying to make sense of from a 6-hour travel distance. Attempting to reassure me, she informed me that she would head to my mother's apartment to try and learn what was going on. Time seemed to be moving both slowly and rapidly, with my mind attempting to fill in pieces like a jigsaw puzzle. Was this it? Had our life novel series finally run its course? Had my favorite story that caused me both joy and pain ended without even a warning? I continued to click on different names on my cell phone, hoping that one would answer and bring me different news.

My mind was fighting within itself as parts of me were in real conflict with the others. I had allowed hope to come back in and seemed to be leading the charge on my hand, whereas the little girl in the corner screaming out seemed to also be getting louder and louder. How could both equally exist? Downstairs my nephew and niece were peacefully sleeping in their beds, and my husband was actively working from his home office with no clue that I was upstairs trying to stop my world from crumbling.

A call came in from my mother's cell phone. Her face emoji is clearly displayed on my screen with her personalized ringtone. I knew I had to answer it, but at that moment, the conflict in my head seemed to just go silent, and I felt completely numb. "Hello, the doctor is here", and … the words no longer mattered. My voice came back, and I let out the loudest explosive wail. She was my mother, but I also felt like I had just lost my child as our roles were often reversed. She was gone, and I knew I would never be the same again. I no longer wanted to be in the driver's seat. My body went into autopilot as I prepared for the burial services and life as I would now know it without her.

My husband runs up the steps as he overhears my cries and is met with a wet yet emotionless face as the words my mom died falls from my lips. I turned around and called different numbers on my phone to tell them the news as I refused to allow them to hear about it on social media. Phone call by phone call, I broke the news calmly, accepted their condolences and words of support and empathy, and provided understanding when they broke down. That overbearing and paralyzing pain had no place right now; my list of things I needed to get done was too long.

SUN

When reflecting on all my experiences, no matter the challenge, I am still here and pushing forward, and I thankfully do not look like everything I made it through. For many, they believed how my story would go; despite the challenges, I have accomplished even more than I initially hoped for. I used to harshly judge myself for not focusing on my education at a young age and how that caused me to have to put in so much work. However, in spite of that, I graduated and went on to earn a Bachelors's and Master's degree. Where I once did not want to give people the opportunity to love me as I feared being hurt again, I have opened myself up to accepting love and trusting people. This has allowed me to be surrounded by a genuine group of people who challenge, love, support, and encourage me. This has helped not only give me the ability to find my voice but also strengthened and trust in it. I have also found forgiveness for myself, my parents, and those who hurt me as it allows me to stop looking backwards in fear but be present and looking forward to the future. I have learned to be kind to myself and take it daily while replaying the tape when needed to remind myself of what I have overcome.

LETTER TO SELF

Hey, Fighter!

If only you could see the woman you have become, you would give yourself more grace now. We have created a life for ourselves that was not even close to what we had envisioned but everything we needed. We did not become talk show hosts; however, our words do provide people with support and guidance while they figure things out. Our love and support for mom never wavered, and we witnessed her growth, sobriety, and authentic self, fully loving and supporting her grandchildren in all the ways we hoped she did for us. Times are difficult now, and there seems to be so much on us that we question how much more we will have to bear or if the next thing will break us. But we make it through. What would have possibly broken many, we learn to mold it into serving us while we write a new chapter. I know life feels unsafe and chaotic right now, but we learn to create ourselves refuge within the storms. You create your own tribe with good solid people who not only support and love with their words but also with their actions. They fully accept you and are continuously building you up.

Their actions break down the walls we had to build and allow trust and love to be fully given to us. The mom you always longed for is found within our mom and bonus mom, who together fill all our prior voids. They both still call us out when needed but also give us that support for growth. Giving space for them allowed us to be open to love with our partner. He is supportive, nurturing, understanding, and kind and knows how to keep us laughing. His love has opened up new dreams and goals for us that we never felt safe enough to consider. You will find understanding and empathy for both our parents, giving so much context to who they are and a real appreciation for them. The most important thing I want to tell you is that you find true safety and create a home for yourself. One that is filled with love reflects our drive and hard work, peaceful, filled with laughter, and safe. You are still learning, reflecting, and growing but have overcome many odds and continue making new strides daily. The cards you were handed early on in life were not the easiest to play, but you have never once left the table and continue to be a force.

CHAPTER ELEVEN

Silent Tears Over The Years

Patricia Williams

I remember being angrier as a child than happy. It wasn't just a wave of normal anger; it was more like red eyes, ears burning, heart rapidly beating angry. Living with my mom made me miserable, and it was never a walk in the park. So let me take you on a short journey of my life.

My mother used to be very disrespectful to me. She would call me every name in the book except for a child of God. It was always a lot of yelling and cursing, no matter what. I never did anything to deserve it. That was just how she communicated with me. I never felt loved by her until my brother passed away in 2015. That was the first time I'd ever heard the words "I love you" from her. "I didn't respond because I didn't love her. How could I love someone who treated me as if I were nothing, making me feel sad, lost, not wanted, and especially not loved? How? She treated me as if she resented me for something or someone doing her wrong. At times I wanted to run away, but I never did.

So, my brother did stay with us until he started getting into trouble too much, and she sent him away to his father in Virginia. He didn't like me much either because he thought our mom loved me more, so he tried to hurt me several times. Thank Goodness he never did. Little did he know; she treated me worse than him in my teenage years. I felt lost when he left. I started disconnecting myself from the world a bit. I was so confused about why God would allow me to go through this type of verbal abuse from someone who was supposed to love and protect me. I was being tortured for whatever reason. I used to pray and ask God,' why? Why would you give me to a mother like this? Why?. I don't remember ever getting an answer.

I felt very lost as a teenager. Of course, I hung out with my cousins, but I wanted a mother-daughter relationship. I wanted and needed to talk to her about my life, but I couldn't. I never saw her smile unless it was at her boyfriend's. She was never really happy when I was around. I didn't know my dad. He was never a part of my life, and at that time, I didn't even know I had four sisters on his side. My life may have been a bit different if I had a relationship with them then, but I didn't, so it was not. I started imagining that my mom resented him so much that she didn't tell me about my sisters. And because I reminded her of him, she mistreated me. I didn't know the real reason, so I made it up.

One day sticks out more than any other; it was the day my life changed forever. I went to a friend's house; at least, I thought he was my friend. I was with my cousins, and I was sexually assaulted. The two people I trusted more than anyone else left me. They were nowhere to be found. I yelled for them to help me. I yelled for him to stop, but no one came, and he kept going. I went into shock and just went numb until he was done. When he stopped and let me go, I walked home slowly, still in shock about what had just happened. No, tears were going down my face, but my heart was crying on the inside. I felt betrayed, lost, broken, scared, and scared. Who do I talk to? Who do I tell? Who's going to believe me? It's my fault! I shouldn't think of went there. I shouldn't have trusted them. These thoughts were going through my mind as the short walk home seemed like one of the longest in my life.

I walked into the house, like a zombie, with blood on my pants and laid on the couch in the fetal position in silence. My mom walked passed me and never acknowledged my presence. I needed my mom. I needed her to hug me. I needed her to tell me it was okay. I needed her to let me scream and cry, but I got nothing. Even when she found out someone had violated me, she did nothing but call the cops. No hugs for me. No kisses. No nothing! I yelled to the cops,' He raped, he raped me,' with tears flowing down my face. It was the worse experience I ever went through in my life, even to this day. So, life was supposed to go on as if nothing ever happened. The friends of my rapist bullied me. My cousins never came to say sorry; my mom never talked about it again. Even to this day, she's never talked to me about it.

My life had shattered and started crumbling. I started skipping school. I even tried to drink one night. I got sicker than my dog, but she still never noticed. I had given up hope of experiencing happiness of any sort. My past took a ride with me in my adulthood. I allowed disrespect and belittlement. Verbal, mental, and physical abuse were my biggest issues. Yet, I got comfortable with them, as if they were my norm. I allowed someone to put his hands on me for four years, and I still loved him.

I felt so broken. My heart was so cold. I no longer wanted to be on earth. I thought about ending it all more times than I should have. Finally, one day I sat in the hallway of our home with a knife clenched in my hand. All sorts of strong thoughts flooded my mind about taking my life: I began crying and screaming. I almost did it! But something stopped me! My kids are what saved me. They became my reason to survive. I had no other reason but to show them what love was. Even though I was learning it through them, I asked myself, "How can you be selfish "and think about leaving your kids alone in this awful world.' "And I just cried. It's not that I didn't love my kids; I didn't love myself enough. I was angry, broken, invalidated, and lost. I had no hopes of ever being found. I just existed for them.

Despite the mask I was hiding behind, I've always been a loving, hardworking person. I pretended to be happy, even when my children were with me. They gave me all the love I had missed, but I still was incomplete. Nothing and no one filled the empty space I had. It was like a hole that ran so deep that no amount of words or things could fill it.

I was very close with my grandma. We even share the same birthday. The relationship between her and me felt so special. I was devastated when God called her home two weeks before my brother passed away. The pain I felt from her death was unimaginable. I was hurt all over again. All I could feel was pain. I remember saying, "When Lord?" "When will this pain stop invading me?" The pain never stopped. My life was like a withered rose with the leaves slowly blackening, falling off one by one, until nothing was left, so it crumbled.

That's what my norm was. The key word is "was" My life started its journey full of sadness, anger, disrespect, loneliness, and especially not Love. However, today, my life is full of love. I'm not as angry and don't deal with disrespect anymore. I had to find my way even though every day was a challenge; It was a challenge I was willing to take. I decided to take my life back and not allow it to disintegrate. I'm living despite all the odds that were against me. My God chose me to be here for a reason. I decided to make him proud of me by finding myself. I will no longer live in the shadows. I never thought I would make it this far, but I have and will.

LETTER TO SELF

Dear Patricia,

You are so loved. Why are you having these bad thoughts. Look at yourself, God made you just as he wanted you to be. He did not make a mistake. it seems like this is the way your mother is going to show you care by being disrespectful but don't think less of yourself. Maybe 'this is the only way she can show you because someone has hurt her, so now she's hurting you. I'm not saying this is the right way to do it. I'm just saying she's never going to change but you can. Stop hiding! Show up in the world. Youve been disguising yourself too long. Stop! Stop feeling like you're not smart enough or beautiful enough. You are all those things and more! You can accomplish anything you put your mind to.

Just Believe in yourself as God does. I know it hurts. I know your lost, I know your heart is cold but baby girl you have your whole life ahead of you. Don't decide to end it now. Put the knife down. Don't step in front of the train. Don't take those pills or drink that alcohol. I promise you that u will get through this. I can't promise that life is going to be just rainbows, but if you fight, I will fight with you and God will strengthen you. He will never leave you as long you keep your faith. You have a purpose, and you will see it sooner than later. You Got this Baby girl. And I got you.

CHAPTER TWELVE

The Search For Self Love

Aja Chrisanta

Until recent years, the various aspects of my life seemed very normal to me, and it was not until I was an adult that I began to realize my childhood environment was anything but normal. I grew up in two different trailers on the same plot, so I lived at the same address for the first 18 years of my life. In both trailers, for some reason or another, there were leaks resulting in moldy, drooping ceilings. Eventually, holes in the floor developed that grew larger and larger until you could see through to the ground below.

The majority of my memories of childhood are that of my parents fighting with one another, oftentimes resulting in my mother throwing items, sometimes aiming for my father's head, and breaking photographs and decorations around the house by throwing them. My mom would usually end up in hysterics, screaming at my dad and us children that she was leaving or was going to kill herself. My sister and I were made aware of our family's financial stress by my parents often, even though, as children, there was nothing we could do to help. My mother was rather busy with work and her social life, and most of the time, I recall feeling as though I had to wait up for her to get home from work for a brief hug and kiss before she left again to go out at night.

I was always called tender-hearted by my family, as I was always quite emotionally sensitive and would often cry for an array of reasons, especially when my parents were fighting. My emotional needs were not often prioritized, and the usual methods used to pacify me were that I was given a snack and put in front of the television, and/or my sister would be asked to supervise me.

I had two sisters, and we were all born with five years passing before the next one. I was the baby of us all. The oldest of my sisters did not live with us but lived with a couple that lived directly across the main highway, so we got to see her rather frequently. She was not my father's daughter biologically, but she never met her biological father, and my father was eager to claim her and love her as his own when she was a baby. She wasn't very nice to me in my earlier years and always bonded more closely with our middle sister. I would later learn that before I was born, she was adopted by this other couple, and although my conception was not expected, my parents brought me into the world and decided to keep the younger two of us in the same household while our oldest sister was living with another family.

Although my live-in sister was only five years older than me, she would often be given the responsibility of watching me, waking me up, and preparing me for school each morning, and when she began driving, she would take me to and from school and work. I adored my sisters and so terribly wanted to feel accepted by both of them as a small child, but they often teased me. At times, I would approach them to interact, only for them to repeatedly shout, "SHUT UP," repeatedly, to make me walk away crying. They succeeded most of the time. Other times, they would assist one another in holding me down and tickling me. It feels embarrassing to admit that this is a painful memory for me.

My sisters would hold me down and tickle me until I was screaming, crying, and ready to vomit. My body was not my own, and my comfort was not a consideration. As I got older, they became kinder to me and tickle-tortured me less frequently. The last time they ever held me down to tickle me was when I was nearing the end of elementary school. We were in the hallway of my eldest sister's apartment that she shared with her boyfriend at the time, but they were acting strange. I had a secret I was trying to maintain and realized that they were inspecting my body part way through. They made their way up my torso, over to my arms, and eventually to my wrists, where I wore wristbands embroidered with logos from my favorite band. My heart was pounding from being tickle-tortured, and in anticipation–There was no way out of this one. They slid the wristbands off and snagged on the scabs of my self-harm. I started crying, and they did too. They pleaded to know why I was harming myself, and I had no explanation at the time.

I wasn't cutting myself to end my life. My emotions would feel so big and overwhelming, and I never felt as though I was allowed to have or express them. After that day, thankfully, they never tickle-tortured me again, and it showed me that they cared about me; however, I would continue to relapse into self-harm and bottle my thoughts and feelings. More frequently at first, then months to years would pass between instances of self-harm, where my methods became easier to hide. I would hit myself on the head where hair grew and could hide the marks. I would dig my nails into my upper arm. I would incessantly scratch my ears and cut my legs and stomach.

Eventually, I would stop these methods of self-harm and find new outlets that turned out to be just as harmful. Emotional neglect is a theme that has followed me throughout life. In the same way, I would await the love I sought from my mother or the acceptance I sought from my sisters. I have done the same in my various relationships in life with friends, colleagues, and romantic partners. Often, I will dismiss or deprioritize my needs in order to be available for others. I also would avoid addressing concerns and needs with people in my life, fearing that if I were unavailable or had created a disruption. I would squander my chances of receiving a display of love, appreciation, or affection. Countless times, I have over-offered myself without prompting to feel needed, wanted, and appreciated.

Strengths that I pride myself in include a mind that is open, patient, understanding, non judgmental, and resourceful, as well as a heart that is loving, nurturing, giving, and helpful. Looking back, it seems that these character attributes stem from the characteristics that the adults in my childhood lacked or withheld. As I navigate adulthood and attempt to build my life, my dreams and aspirations have ultimately become to love myself entirely in every aspect and to be a successful esthetician living in financial freedom. Unfortunately, although these goals are achievable, I find myself jumping self-imposed hurdles of poor body image, low motivation, poor discipline, easy distraction, and a looming sense of inferiority to those around me.

Throughout my journey, the most influential people have been my immediate family—my mother, father, and older sisters—as well as my friends, romantic partners, and the children of my romantic partners. Due to my childhood experiences and the adults around me during that chapter of life, I try to be present, available, and gentle and do everything within my means for the children of my romantic partners. I feel a sense of responsibility and urgency to ensure that I am not creating or contributing to an emotionally neglectful childhood for them. The children I have had the pleasure of becoming a bonus parent have become the bonus loves of my life and a chance to love a little human wholesomely.

These people have taught me imperative lessons on how to be and how not to be. As I previously shared, my older sister was integral to my childhood. As she grew up, she also had to share a part-time duty to raise me, especially after my mother left. At that time, I was 12, and my older sisters were 17 and 23. My eldest sister was already out in the world building her own life, so we naturally saw her less frequently. Following our mother's exit, the sister I lived with really began allowing me to spend more time with her. She taught me HTML coding at the dawn of social media, attempted to teach me about social justice, and created the outline of my music and film taste. Regardless of the activity, she always made sure to make me feel included and wanted–even if it was evident she did not want to.

Once I reached my preteen into my teenage years, she included me when hanging out with her friends. There was no cooler experience at the time, especially since I struggled to maintain ongoing friendships. While fun, these regular interactions with older teenagers and young adults began exposing me to various experiences and interests. I began smoking cigarettes and marijuana, drinking alcohol and seeking the attention of boys. The use of substances were modeled in my home, and eventually, my sister and father stopped scolding me and decided it was safer that I do so at home or with my sister nearby than to be out on my own doing so.

I began receiving the attention I wanted from teenage boys and grown men as I began spending more time away from home in questionable social settings. My sister would be vocal in her disagreement with this and would try to speak to me about it. I never wanted to hear about it. Looking back, I realize she wanted to protect me. I wish I had listened. Between the age of 12, until I became an adult, I became hypersexual, and the majority of my sexual interactions were non-consensual, as they were typically an adult, and I was typically heavily intoxicated.

During the years 2010 and 2011, we spent our time at a man's house that was always the go-to spot for partying. I was so engulfed in the happiness I felt that this seemingly cultured, funny interior design aficionado with quite the knowledge of indie films wanted to hang out with me all the time. It was not until I was 25 years old that I realized how predatory our dynamic was. My mother was living with her new husband at the time of my sixteenth birthday, and she bought me a keg and wheeled it into this man's house for my birthday party. As a teenager, I was grateful that she wanted to be a friend and enabler more than a mother; however, as an adult, it made me terribly sad. This man would use me at ages 15 and 16 to bring men and underage boys alike to his parties. Sometimes he specifically took me to his bedroom or bathroom during the parties to engage in sexual acts so that he could masturbate next to us or join in with us.

One evening I was in and out of consciousness and recalled him helping me up off the couch with another man. He took me up to the attic of the house, and the next time I recall opening my eyes, I was mid-rape at the hand of this friend of his that helped bring me to the attic. I learned from another friend of mine that he had been forcibly raped by my abuser as well. A few months later, I was sitting in a large park sharing this experience with a friend while we awaited the start of a protest, and she turned to me in horror. A few months following that instance, a man posted on social media about being manipulated and raped by my abuser with the assistance of another drug-addicted woman. The posting described a scenario identical to those I had been in.

My abuser was boldly commenting how the poster enjoyed it. I never came forward in a public manner about this individual, or any of the individuals that are pedophiles and/or rapists, out of fear and unwillingness to put myself in the line of fire. Almost all of these men are rumored in our local area to have committed some form of sexual violence. Still, I see people who outwardly praise their characters and still hang out with them, and I am simply not ready to consider coming forward with any of these individuals.

During this same time, our uncle had an accident that resulted in an absurdly generous opioid pain pill prescription, which he then commissioned my sister to sell for him. We began selling and abusing the pills together, as well as separately. Around this time, my father became addicted to a synthetic drug that was easily obtainable at gas stations and tobacco stores. He became extremely aggressive, combative, paranoid, and generally frightening to be around. Once it was deemed illegal, he had no choice but to quit. It was a very brief time, but I remember it as the scariest my father had ever been. With irritability being a common side effect of drug abuse, all of us drifted apart more than we ever had. By the time my senior year of high school arrived, my uncle had stopped giving his prescription to us to sell, and pills had become extremely difficult and expensive to obtain without a prescription. In a moment of desperation to use, I was introduced to heroin, and it changed absolutely everything.

At the time, it felt like a blessing! It was less expensive, it was stronger, and it was very easy to find. One morning before school, I left my sister a sticky note and three baggies of heroin, thinking that I was offering a kind and thoughtful gesture. By the springtime of 2012, I had become involved with a boy close to my age, with whom I connected over our shared interest in drugs. Our relationship immediately became one of codependence, obsession, and toxicity. He was dealing drugs out of his mother's house, and I would often skip school to hang out with him, and it was one of those days that I received my first drug charge. The police confiscated all of my drugs and paraphernalia. As the police were entering me into the criminal system, they made me aware that I needed to notify my school.

I was kicked out of high school just a few months shy of graduation. As the moments passed, physical withdrawal symptoms were appearing at a greater severity and speed than I had ever experienced. I remember placing my hands on the wall behind the toilet, my feet on the wall in front of it, and not being able to gain control over my body. Incessant heaving even after my stomach was completely vacant, muscle spasms and sensations of extreme heat and cold over my entire body. My sister was trying desperately to help me find a small amount of any kind of opioid so that I wasn't in such great pain. We finally found some relief, and I went down for a nap on the couch, only to have my dad wake me up and notify me that I needed to get my things together because he was taking me to rehab in Baltimore.

I only spent a week in rehab. Our medical insurance only covered detox services. At a visit with my mom and sister, they let me know I was going to be leaving so soon, and I was over the moon. I remember the look of concern and fright on my mother and sister's faces. When I arrived back home, I spent time with my boyfriend and our friends that were still using, and I lasted maybe two weeks before I relapsed. It isn't entirely clear to me if my sister was still using during this time, but eventually, we began using together. Our oldest sister was living in another state at the time and told me I was not allowed to be a part of her and her children's lives if I was not willing to stop using drugs. It hurt me deeply, but not deep enough for me to stop.

During the next two years, my sister, who raised me, nearly became a stranger, only crossing paths if I stopped by the trailer to use or make a sale. Both of our addictions progressed rapidly, and we did many things we said we'd never do to get more drugs. I experienced several sexual traumas in addiction, which I had dismissed at the time because I was addicted to drugs and prostituting. I simply assumed it was to be expected. In an attempt to straighten up her life, my sister decided to move to Ohio with our mother when our father lost our childhood trailer. Shortly before the move, I learned I was pregnant. I was not sure how far along I was because using altered my cycle, and I was too intoxicated most of the time to notice the outward changes.

Just a few days after arriving in Ohio, my drugs ran out, and I was going through extreme physical withdrawal symptoms, perhaps the worst I had ever experienced. I remember laying in my mother's shower for nearly an entire day because it was easier to just turn the water on every time I vomited or defecated than to try and move my weak body to the bathroom. My mother tried to convince me to stay there and quit cold turkey, but I was not interested and quickly made arrangements to take a train back home.

Once home, my father took me to terminate the pregnancy. I continued using for several more months, finding lower lows, adding new drugs to my list of substance dependencies, prostituting, becoming suicidal, and frequently found myself in trouble with the police. Once I reached the holiday season at the end of 2013, I was just broken. I was so terrified of trying to get clean because of how physically, mentally, and emotionally painful it was, and I didn't want to live any longer.

A few days into January of 2014, I checked myself into detox again. The boyfriend I used drugs with broke up with me, and from that point forward started attending 12-step meetings. I was 19 years old and very altered by living the life of an addict. Prior to this, I had overstayed my welcome in every place I tried to go. The 12-step fellowship was such a strange place and full of people I was not sure about, but they made me feel welcome, wanted, and loved–all feelings I have always craved so deeply. My experience in 12-step meetings became chaotic quickly. I ended up swiftly entering a relationship with a man 20 years older than me and disliked by many people in attendance because he had cheated on and left another member of the fellowship to be with me.

Once again, I felt a lack of acceptance from those around me, particularly the women who attended meetings. I continued going despite the palpable tension and dove into service work for the program under the wing of a woman who had been clean for several years. I was told by many members that we must give in the form of being of service in order to keep what was given to me–a chance at living clean. This did not go over well with me. I began to spend all of my free time in church basements and spent many years riddled with anxiety trying to find balance.

My relationship with the older man was rather codependent, much like my previous relationships, but something was distinctly different this time. On the one hand, it was the happiest romantic relationship I had ever been in, probably because it was the first one I was in without the factor of drug use involved. On the other hand, I feel that this relationship was more detrimental to how I viewed myself than any other relationship I had been in. There would be times that we would be amongst friends, and I would make a joke, and our friends would be laughing. He stood nearby and shook his head at me, later telling me that what I said was not funny. He would praise me and my appearance sometimes, then turn around and pick my appearance apart, criticizing my outfit choices in regard to my body size and shape. He would tell me certain meals I'd eat were going to undo all of the work I had done at the gym.

In 2016, I celebrated two years clean. By this point, I wasn't attending as many meetings because I was working and attending classes at a local community college. In 12-step meetings, yearly milestones are a big deal and are encouraged to be celebrated. On my anniversary, I decided to start attending meetings more. Nine days after my anniversary, I went to a later evening meeting on a Saturday, and I spent considerable time in the parking lot afterward talking with other members. I remember driving home feeling pleased with my choice to do so and feeling good about participating in the fellowship. I arrived at the house, went upstairs to my boyfriend, chatted with him for a moment, and hopped in the shower. When I got out of the shower, I had a missed call from my sister's boyfriend in Ohio that I initially didn't deem urgent, but he followed with a message that I needed to call him back immediately. I figured she had been arrested and put back in jail again.

During the two years I spent staying clean, my sister had been struggling to do so. She would do okay for a few weeks here and there, and her boyfriend would contact me and let me know she was acting suspicious again or that he had evidence she was using. My body was still damp, my hair was still dripping, and I was in my towel still. The air against my damp skin, alongside anticipation, was giving me shivers and goosebumps. I called him back, and he told me to sit down. I sat on my chair in the corner of the room that I shared with my boyfriend. My heart was pounding, and I could hear it in both of my ears. I was breathing shakily, awaiting whatever would come out of his mouth next. "Your sister is dead." The air left my body, my body met the floor, and I could do nothing but bawl.

I remember my boyfriend's elderly grandmother banging on his door, begging him to stop hurting me because she thought he was beating me. I had to call my father. I did not want to, but I had to. I honestly hoped he wouldn't pick up the call. He was always due to work early in the morning; by this time, it was late in the evening. He picked up the call, and I somehow mustered the words to notify him of her death. He fell apart on the other end of the call, and I couldn't get a response. I could just hear him falling apart. I turned to my boyfriend and said, "I need to go home."

He drove me home, about 15 minutes away, in silence. I just wept in the passenger seat. Once I arrived at my grandparents, where my father lived, we decided to call my oldest sister together. She was living in Texas at the time. She sobbed, and it was searing. Eventually, my dad and I made our way to bed to get a few hours of sleep. My grandparents would wake up in a few hours, and we needed to tell them the terrible news. I remember coming down the stairs, and they were so excited I had joined them for breakfast on a Sunday morning. I went and sat on the couch, and my dad stood in the living room between me and the television. They were setting the table, making extra space for me. My dad broke the news to them, and I saw my grandparents sob for the first time ever.

They spent much of Brittney's childhood with her, and always ensured that our family never went without. I reached out to a close friend, and we went to a 12-step meeting together and got food afterward. I felt guilty for doing absolutely anything at all because my sister could no longer do anything. Everything felt wrong. I was swelling with regret and grief with every thought that passed through my mind. I was not as warm with her as I felt I should have been in the months leading up to her death. I was very devoted to the program that I was working to stay clean, and I was so adamant and militant with her, until I was fed up.

Once I was fed up, my responses became shorter, and we did not speak much at all in the weeks leading up to her passing.

I told her she was going to die if she kept using, and I knew that it was a possibility for any person using drugs, but for some reason, I just did not believe it would happen to her. In just a few weeks, she was supposed to move back to Delaware, and I still sit wondering if she would be alive today if she had just made it here. She often expressed how lonely and sad she was, and it ate away at me to know that she was lonely in life and alone when she died. She overdosed in a basement with just her four pets. My oldest sister flew in nearly immediately, and my father left for Ohio to support my mother and grieve with her.

My mother described to me in detail the state she was in, and my father offered me a photograph of her on the cadaver, which I declined. Although I never viewed my sister after her passing, the imagery of my mother's description is an intrusive thought and mental image still to this day, over six years later. For several months following her death, I spent a lot of my days in a trance-like state, with frequent bouts of easily triggered emotional overwhelm. How was I supposed to keep living and breathing?-Even in the moments where it was not challenging to do so, I had such nagging guilt for surviving her death, and existing felt like a chore. I lived with a lump in my throat that seemed to stick around no matter what I was focused on and a tight, burning sensation in my chest. It was such complex guilt I buried myself in. Not only did I have the opportunity to stay clean and continue living, she never got a chance to experience real freedom from addiction.

Although stunting in many ways, I perceive the loss of my sister as a pivotal moment in my life. I did not want to feel anything, but it shattered every illusion I had about ever going back to using the substances I once took comfort in. The only way out was through the feelings. I began analyzing the relationships I was maintaining and the amount of effort I was giving these relationships. Within 11 months of my sister's death, I ended the relationship I had with my boyfriend, sought out a new job, and began to pay attention to my tendency to people-please. In that first year, it occurred to me that I had been using people-pleasing as a manipulative tactic to secure their acceptance and love. The next revelation was that I was going above and beyond to secure the love and acceptance of people who did not reciprocate my efforts. Ultimately, it was the beginning of an ongoing journey of trying to love myself enough not to settle for crumbs of love from others.

My grandfather died just over a year after my sister, and toward the end of his life, we did not get along well. I began to expand my awareness of societal and political issues and determine my morals and values. As my awareness grew, I became aware that my grandfather was outwardly racist, and I was becoming increasingly outspoken and combative. On his deathbed, I was able to have the hospital room to myself for a moment, and I don't know if he could hear me, but I apologized for my part in our tensions. I was very triggered by racism coming from my family members on both sides of the family. My mother's side is from the Philippines, and my father's side is from North Carolina. I was neither Filipino enough to feel validated by the maternal side of my family nor was I Caucasian enough to feel validated by my paternal grandfather. I realize now pertaining to this, that I am whole in my mixedness, and although there were racially-charged aggressions present in my family, these same people also managed to make sure my parents and their children never went without the necessities.

When I left detox the last time, my grandfather welcomed me into their home with open arms and a lot of assistance getting back on my feet. He was always my biggest cheerleader, especially with my academic achievements, and he always did anything within his means to give me a chance to be great. I suffered with a lot of guilt about my words and actions toward him in his last year of life, but I have since been able to make peace with the fact that I can inherently disagree with some of his stances and views but still love and appreciate him and the love and safety he provided me throughout life.

The partners and environments I chose began to have higher standards to meet, but I still struggled with enforcing my standards and boundaries and continued dismissing red-flag behaviors for a while. I found a better-paying job and someone who was kinder and more affectionate to me than all of my previous partners, and we eventually moved in together along with another couple–my best friend and their partner. I was content with the dynamic for some time and relished being in a space that I could partially call my own, where I had some say in the household and could find privacy when I required it. Then, 2020 began. 2020 was a transformative year that shook things up.

The pandemic began, and 12-step meetings went virtual. Leading up to this point, I had been of service for the fellowship as chairperson for several subcommittees and eventually as the area's chairperson. At that time, I began to see a lot of egos battling and a lot of people with decades of abstinence acting as emotionally immature as the newcomers. I was already quite exhausted with my efforts of service and began to lessen my meeting attendance and service commitments.

After over seven years of feeling loved and accepted by rooms full of people, I suddenly felt very alone. The people I was trying to maintain relationships with were not reciprocating in the capacity they once would, and I was no longer feeling the constant outpouring of love. My best friend and I began participating in activism more, and both of our live-in partners were disinterested in this passion of ours. It became clear to me that my partner was not on the same page with the issues I felt compelled to protest, and he became unsupportive and condescending toward our activism group and me.

Our activism group was arrested with excessive force and made some local headlines, and those comments were from people who I looked up to and formed friendships with, saying hurtful things like the police should have shot us or that people driving in the area of our protest should have run us over with their vehicles. I became enraged and severed my association with the fellowship entirely. My best friend and their partner separated shortly after due to a lack of empathy and support from the partner, and the house was down to three tenants. I dismissed my partner's disagreements for several months and tried to maintain the relationship. I feared that no one would ever love me and be as unproblematic as a romantic partner. I proposed we begin looking at moving out of the state, as I was ready to spread my wings and broaden my horizons, and it was not something they were willing to even consider.

Eventually, we moved another housemate in; they were a friend of mine. The household shifted from comfortable and homelike to volatile, aggressive, and tense. Our new housemate was treating my best friend very poorly, and my partner had joined in. My partner and new housemate began spending a lot of time together while I worked, and I had an inclination that the two were gravitating toward one another. Their chemistry was noticeable to my best friend and me. I was panicking for a very short time and began experiencing anger, jealousy, inferiority, and sadness. I realized I did not actually care whether or not my partner was falling in love with someone else; I wasn't in love with my partner anymore and hadn't been for a long time. I was clinging to familiarity and normalcy. I ended the relationship about seven weeks into the new 4-person living dynamic. It was then decided by the two of them that I should move out when originally my two friends and I were going to remain in the house and my ex-partner would be the one to leave.

I moved out and into another part of the state that I was unfamiliar with, in a temporary arrangement with someone I was acquainted with from work to get my finances in order so that I could move to the opposite coast in half a year. Unexpectedly, the chemistry was intense, and I was head over heels for someone new within just a few weeks. I was fantasizing about and discussing the long-term future with a partner for the first time. I felt seen, loved, respected, and adored to a new depth I never knew before. They have three children that I co-parented alongside their mother and father.

For the first time ever, I was engaged to be married. Life was amazing, and I had a family and children I could pour love and affirmation into. I found such solace in my new purpose–to be a wife and bonus mother to four people I love immensely. Things were not perfect, but they were wonderful and fulfilling. The only thing I wanted to change about my life at the time was my career. I had gone my entire working life uncertain of what field I wanted to devote my working hours too until around this time. I quit my job with a lack of thorough preparation but felt confident in my choice because I talked it over with my fiancé and had their word of support in whatever I chose to do, including whether I went to school full-time or part-time. I opted to begin full-time classes because I would graduate in fewer months and be able to contribute financially to my household sooner by doing so. Tensions were higher in the household but did not seem unmanageable. Two weeks into my new studies, I came home from school, having just done a full face of makeup with my new equipment and skills. I felt beautiful, which was not a frequent occurrence for me. My fiancé complimented how beautiful I looked and said we needed to talk about something.

He broke off the engagement and told me he could not see a future with me because of my selfish decision-making. Similarly, to when I received the call about my sister's death, I found myself on the floor in disbelief and indescribable emotional pain and confusion. Behind these decisions, my goals for happiness and fulfillment were indeed at the forefront, but part of that fulfillment would be my ability to provide for our home and children. We continued living together for a few months until he eventually felt he needed more space. I moved back in with my family, and we maintained a relationship with more space and time than we previously had; however, I was grateful for the few nights a week I could spend in my old home, trying my best to pretend everything was fine.

I spent several months with swollen eyes and second guesses about myself. Constantly, I worried about what I could do to fix this and how I could make my way back home. I began punching myself in the head and digging my nails into my arms again when my fear and sadness was too overwhelming. I felt like a failure. I felt unlovable. I felt abandoned. I became insecure on the nights we didn't spend together and was told by my ex-fiancé that it was not their responsibility to manage my insecurities, and they were correct. I took the concerns I had about myself to my therapist and tried to work diligently to be more emotionally stable, as I did not want to squander my chances of earning my place back in the family and home. Over several months, things improved, the tension was low, and my insecurities were hushed. I felt confident we were both working toward coming back together. They were apologetic for making me feel as though I had done anything wrong to cause the split, and communication was returning to a healthier, less combative place. I was exhausted, but the fight for what or who I love is a worthwhile fight.

My birthday was the day before I graduated school, and due to our busy schedules and our current financial problems, we did not celebrate my birthday or graduation together. I was sad but brushed it off as a worthy sacrifice. We were both chipping away at our individual goals. Things continued to improve, and my confidence was returning. A few months later, it was a long Sunday with the children, after which I decided to do side work delivering food for several hours, returning to the house at 1 o'clock in the morning. My drive back home was about an hour long, and I was exhausted and asked if it would be okay if I stayed one more night. To my surprise, my ex-fiancé was extremely upset with my request and expressed that they did not feel I was respecting their boundaries or request for space. I felt hurt by the lack of consideration for my exhaustion, and we were discussing the issue at hand when they suddenly darted out the front door.

I was confused and genuinely scared of what may be happening outside, so I stayed inside. Several minutes later, they storm in, stomping and breathing heavily, stating, "we need to talk about some shit." They had an angry visitor. Another partner that I was unaware of had come to the house, saw my car, and they argued. My ex-fiancé let me know that after I moved out, they began having sex with an ex-partner that I had never heard of before. This partner had unexpectedly conceived a baby and subsequently paid for an abortion. On the floor, again. I was willing to keep working on myself with my therapist if my ex-fiancé was willing to keep working on themself. I was still clinging to the goal of marrying them and assimilating once again to living under the same roof and raising their children.

Within a few weeks, I found myself unable to get out of bed until absolutely necessary, disinterested in everything, perpetually nauseous, and unable to look in the mirror. Why am I so difficult to love? Why am I not enough? Why does each person I love abandon me in some way, time and time again? I expressed concern about the amount of reassurance and commitment I would require in order to not be enveloped in insecurity, which was much more than they had expressed wanting to provide initially in the breakup, with hopes that they would choose to try to work on the relationship with me.

The person I perceived to be the love of my life, my one and only, looked me in the eyes and told me they did not have the capacity or willingness to nurture my emotional needs. Finally, I heard not only their words but saw their actions loud and crystal clear. Once again, I had spent at least the duration of our undefined situationship dismissing my needs and desires to keep someone with me. I was abandoning myself in an attempt to have someone change their mind about abandoning me. I spent months neglecting myself. I had overstepped my own boundaries and waived my own standards to keep someone who was causing me immense pain comfortable instead of pouring the love and effort into myself, with hope and expectation that one day my life could return to how things were with that person before things fell apart. Although proud of my growth and progress, I struggled to find the compassionate, patient love for myself that I had so happily poured into another person. I poured from a long-empty cup and had nothing left for myself, which ended up being of great detriment to my perception of self.

Despite the traumas, trials, and tribulations I have seen, working hand in hand with my poor, distorted perception of self, I now look back on so many accomplishments that I have previously minimized or not given myself due credit for. It is a miracle that I was able to get clean and remain abstinent from hard drugs. I went to college and graduated cum laude with an Associate's degree in Business. I took a leap of faith and quit a lucrative yet unfulfilling job to pursue my dreams by enrolling in a trade program for esthetics, graduating with academic achievement and attendance awards, then passing both of my licensure examinations with high scores. I was granted a pardon by the Governor for my felony criminal record and was able to then have my entire criminal background expunged and removed from the criminal database. My living sister and I have formed a deep, strong bond and crave one another's company. I have forgiven my parents and come to understand that they, too, have been traumatized by their lives. Just this year, I learned more of the sexual traumas my mother endured throughout her life, the substance abuse my parents struggled with when I was a child, and my mother was recently diagnosed with some mental illnesses that explain a lot of her behaviors and patterns. Most importantly of all, I was able to survive all of my trauma thus far and have genuinely thrived in spite of it. I feel as though my greatest accomplishments will be the ones that occur within me mentally, emotionally, and spiritually. I can feel my perception of myself becoming less distorted the more I work on improving the areas of myself that I want to, with self-love as my motivator and intention.

LETTER TO SELF

To all my precious, former selves:

I know that being you does not feel right. It seems like everyone is frustrated and short with you more often than not.

No one has the time or space for any of your needs, and you feel like an annoyance, a burden, or an afterthought to everyone who is supposed to love you. You spend most of your time in fantastical daydreams of another life, another body, another world. I know how deeply you crave a sense of comfort, and unfortunately, you'll spend your entire childhood and several years of adulthood, looking for that comfort in substances and other people. You have overcome so many situations, and obstacles meant to break you. No matter what life has thrown your way, you keep surviving. You PREVAIL. So many people will be drawn to your gentle, empathetic spirit and tender heart, and many of them will drain you. You have been neglected, abandoned, manipulated, abused, taken for granted, hurt, hurt, hurt...yet you still remain kind-hearted. You curse this kind heart and wish you could be more cold, calloused, unphased.

DO NOT allow yourself to grow cold, calloused, unphased. Your tenderness, despite the cruelty, is your superpower. Through all of the trials and tribulations, you are constantly working on self-improvement, and I am SO proud of you. You may not see the light at the end of whichever tunnel you may be in currently, but I promise the effort is worth it. You will endure some terrible storms in life, but you will accomplish so much. You are neurodivergent, and that honestly contributes to so many reasons why you are incredible! How others have treated you at every phase of your life has caused you to see yourself with cruel, unkind eyes. You often feel ugly, small, undesirable, unlovable, inferior, annoying, and burdensome. These feelings could not be further from the truth. You are beautiful, amazing, worthy of love, competent, interesting, helpful, kind, insightful, smart, compassionate, and give so much love to so many people. There is nothing wrong with you besides the people you have allowed to influence your self-image and self-perception. You are worth every single ounce of love and effort you have given away to people, and you deserve double the love and effort back that you have given to people who do not reciprocate. There is no one like you in this world. You are so special, and YOU ARE WORTHY.

I love you so much,
You.

CHAPTER THIRTEEN

Triumph Over Trauma

Victoria Ross

As the eldest of three children to a single mother, I was also the "mommy sister." I did everything a mother would do, from helping with homework to even cooking dinner when my mom was at work. While I acted as the mommy sister, I was under the rule of a woman with an iron fist. There were crazy rules, strict rules, and rules for the rules. Every time I thought about being a jubilant and jovial child, I was reminded of the rules I could have broken and the consequences. Our house was strict, and we knew there would be consequences for anything you wanted to do or thought about doing.

As we grew older, I was also introduced to transparency. At a young age, I knew "what happens in this house stays in this house. Nothing that happened here was to go outside of those doors." The queen had spoken, and I knew she meant that. There were often times when "don't be in these streets telling those white folks our business" echoed in my mind. I was quick on my feet, but this one time in middle school, I was pulled out of class and ushered into a small office. I was scared! What did I do? Had I done anything? My mom would be vexed if she knew I was pulled from class and not doing my work.

But there I was met by a woman. She was short, thin, blonde with light blue eyes. I could never forget how she looked through me and tried to trick me into telling her what was happening in my house. I was quicker than her; I was smart. She will never know. She went through a list of questions about what to do in a fire and who got me ready for school. She even asked who lived in my home. In my mind, I remembered what my momma told me "don't be having those white folks in our business" I heard a voice in my head "lady, you know I'm not telling you anything. I was taught early on that white folks will smile in your face, get what they want and use it against you, tear your family apart and put you in a foster home. But I was smart, well smarter than her, to say the least. My mom gets me ready, I'm never my sister's caretaker, but I do know how to cook and call for help if I never need to.

While in the home of strict rules & lack of transparency, we were never allowed to be sad. We had no reason, right? We did have a home, clean clothes, and food readily available. So why would you feel sadness in a home where resources were not plentiful? It was a single mother's home with 1 of my two siblings. We shared a small bedroom that my mom worked so hard to provide. She worked tirelessly to provide and meet our basic needs. My first experience with sadness was at my high school graduation. I graduated with honors. I was the one in the family to break the high school dropout stigma. I made it. As I walked across the stage, I felt success resting in my chest.

After walking across the stage, I did what every graduate did. I went to look for my mom. Where was she? I just graduated. She was in the car in the parking lot. I asked, "hey are we going to take pictures?". She said, "NO, I don't want to get stuck in traffic." She spoke in such a matter-of-fact tone that I swallowed my happiness and joy. I smiled and said, "OK." I thought this would be important. She had never graduated high school, let alone college. I knew this would be celebrated as an accomplishment. I was crushed but smiled through the disappointment. My mom would never say I'm proud of you or congratulations because this is what I was supposed to do. We don't celebrate the bare minimum. It was the expectation.

It was difficult growing up in a home where you never were celebrated. It created a defeatist attitude because the outcome would always be the same win, lose or draw. You did just what you were supposed to do. You were constantly reminded that we were never allowed to show sadness. It was internal, bottled, ready to explode and flow like the Niger river. You had a home, food, and clothes. Why were you sad? I was sad. I succeeded, and it wasn't recognized. Not knowing what was next were there college applications, apartments, a job or just run away from this life? These are conversations that my mother never had with me. I needed support. I was an eighteen-year-old graduate, just starting her adult life in the world. I felt like I was utterly alone

History repeated itself when it was time to graduate college. I thought, "This time, this was going to be different." I finally graduated college. I can't believe I'm a first again. I made it across the stage with exclamations, cheers, smiles hugs. My grandma even made it this time. My mommy and granny are here to support me. I thought to myself, "This is going to be different." "I know she's going to be waiting for me." "I know she's proud of what I've done." Wait"! "Where was she"? "She wasn't here"? I couldn't find her. "Wait, I know where she is ......in that damn parking lot." She wasn't in the car this time but waiting by the gate, looking to make a dash for it. I saw her. My mom, my grandma and my sister with flowers. I got flowers. My mom bought me flowers this time, but she looked rushed. I asked her are you going somewhere? Her response was ....home, there are too many people here.

I guess this was just another layer to being the strong woman she was. I've never seen this woman cry, ask for help or even be vulnerable enough to ask for help. That's how I knew to be strong. Strong in my house, with my mother, was doing it all yourself, even if it meant shutting others out of your reality. That was strength !!! That was a strength? How was I to know what being weak and rebuilding yourself from the deepest darkest cave filled with depression was? How could I say I was strong If I had never seen weakness? I never really could verbalize or visualize a strong woman, but I knew my mom had to be it. I mean, how could she not? She ruled her house alone with an iron fist, and there was no room for error. But maybe she wasn't strong at all. I watched for over 15 years as she chose a man who didn't choose her.

He was her weakness. Then and only then could I even see her with disappointment after each letdown she endured. Time and time again, I saw him wearing her down. She let a man who had disappointed not only her but her beloved girls. That man made promises.He promised us cars and even a house this one time I remember the house because it was a dream to have my own room and get out of that boring apartment. His lies were elaborate, conniving, and even diabolical. I think he thrived on breaking hearts and making people need him. Because I never had my biological father in my life, he was who I looked up to.

But he also helped me to grow a distrust for men. He let me down from the after-school pick-ups he missed, giving me my first heartbreak, to the lies he created about why he couldn't get me the car we picked out and test drove that was all set to be delivered on my birthday.

As I grew older and wiser, I soon realized that all men weren't like him. All men didn't have two families that lived less than five miles from each other. All men weren't horrible, just him. Their long ongoing situation made my mother's strength even clearer. She was a woman on her own, doing the best she could. The lies and deceit she endured in her love life made her callous, cold, and strong because she depended on herself. She only had herself. It wasn't until I could break down and cry to a complete stranger that I felt strong, powerful, grand, and accomplished. I embraced my weaknesses and used them as strengths.

We didn't have a lot of celebrations or even birthday parties because we never had excess money to waste on a birthday that would happen again next year. She did try to acknowledge my 13th birthday. She wasn't home when I got home from school, that wasn't unusual, but had made me a cake. It was a yellow cake with white icing. And next to it was an envelope with a handwritten note "Happy birthday, don't forget to vacuum and fix you and your sister some dinner." She tried, and

I was acknowledged for turning another year wiser and another year older. But without the big fancy parties, I always had my faith.

My grandmother was a praying woman. She was the most spiritual, saved, and sanctified woman I knew. She had a scripture for everything. I mean a scripture for scripture, a scripture for why my red lipstick wasn't allowed, and only trollops wore red nails. If I skinned my knee, let's pray about it. If my head was hurting, we would pray about it. When my grandfather died, she reminded the family, "he's with the good Lord now" Every thanksgiving, it was my duty to make sure she knew I knew the word. I said to her, "mom mom I'm ready this year to read my scripture." She would look at me with the eyes of the good Lord God himself and say "all right now, Vic....let me hear it" I would give her the smile of a saint and say, "Jesus wept. "she would roll her eyes and remind me, "at least you know something." I loved her and her constant prayers and scriptures. For her, I'm thankful, and I try daily to live righteously with the faith she spent her life installing in her favorite granddaughter. ME! It wasn't until my daughter died that my world began to shift as well as my faith. My daughter died; I'll be fine. The Lord makes no mistakes. Or does he? When devastation struck my household, I didn't know where to turn. Had the almighty good Lord that does all things left me? Did he betray me by taking my child? That's not faith, or is it? I questioned all that I knew—even doubting his existence. If God didn't exist, where could my daughter be? Was she floating in the clouds? A part of me knew the truth and those bible studies followed by six-day services and two Sunday services stuck with me. I know God. I know his faith. My healing is proof of his love—my faith. Hmm, I'm still unsure, and shaken, but I do know there is a god. God wrapped his arms around me when I didn't think I could push on. Amen, and thank you to my grandmother, who made sure I would have a belief system to carry me when I couldn't carry myself.

While my grandmother spent most of her life loving those around her and the community, my home life was completely different. I never heard I love you or you're doing a good job. Do you know what your mother's hug feels like? Does her voice echo "I love you" in your brain when you feel alone? Do you know her voice when it's filled with admiration, pride, and joy? I can't even imagine the love those things can bring. Yet, I am the eldest, the prodigy, the golden child, "mommy sister" that has never been celebrated or supported; physically, emotionally, or financially.

I've been affected in a way that caused me to isolate, shut down, and almost abandon my motherly maternal instincts. I even felt like abandoning my true self, my feelings at times, and my happiness to create and perpetuate the strong black woman stereotype. I wanted to show I was strong and didn't cry or even need anyone to comfort me. I began to wear my mask on April 28, 2018. That was the day my life changed forever.

It was a beautiful sunny day. I'm doing my typical eight-month waddle down the stairs to enjoy my ritual pre-appointment orange juice. Avery was a lazy baby that would either be super active or utterly lazy and sleep through appointments. She definitely was her mother's child. Orange juice woke her up and made it easier for the ultrasound techs to gather the information they needed for the day." Alright, Avery, it's show time." I stood in the mirror, caressing my tight and hard belly, admiring the life I was growing. Wow, birds were singing in the background. They knew the joy in my heart. Oh my god, I just realized I woke up without being nauseous. I knew that day was going to be nothing short of amazing. I sighed and thought, "we are getting to the end. I finally am getting the relief I've needed". I uncapped my minty toothpaste. I heard the water running, and my son moved in his bed. I thought, "Today is going to be a good day." As I got dressed, I pulled my blue denim-like hot girl maternity pants over my belly. They were snug, but I only had a couple more weeks to wear them. I'll be fine.

It's baby check day. These appointments became so routine I could be my own doctor. So on the elevator, I went. It was romantically lit, almost like I was going to a fancy dinner, but it made the ride relaxing. It was eerily quiet, but typically I would have been there yesterday. I thought to myself, "maybe, "I should change these last few appointments to Thursdays if it's going to be this calm." "But Nah, my husband wouldn't make it if I did that." I felt a buzz in my pocket. Ahh, hubby called to check in just before I hit the reception area. It was a typical conversation that ended with the typical I Love You, but I'm going to eat before heading to work. Avery was calm, still, and off of routine. I did my pre-appointment checklist; prenatal vitamins? Check. Water? Check. Orange Juice? Check... I forgot my baby aspirin...I knew I had forgotten something. Damn it!!! I have some in the car; I'll take them when I leave.

The reception area was bustling with children, baby bellies, and the faint chatter between parents. Everyone was happy, smiling faces of strangers always calmed an anxious mind. Mrs. Ross, room 4! Oh my God, this baby must weigh 50 pounds. The bowling ball on my bladder set a time limit between seeing my baby and the bathroom. Oh well, I'll wait. I entered the Darkroom, but it was soothing. The temperature was just right to take a quick nap once we started. The dimly lit room had a few monitors and screens acting as ambient lighting. Click, click, tap, tap. She's rolling her chair back and forth between screen and charts. Click, click, tap, tap. I could hear the other rooms' doors open and shut in the hallway. Alright, let's check on this little baby. That was my favorite part of every appointment. I gleamed from ear to ear. Yay!! This is going to be good. I wonder what she weighs now. Is she still sleeping? I closed my eyes, and the warm gel began to glide back and forth across my belly. I look up at the screen directly in front of me. The time reads 2:14 pm. A little more gliding and a couple more pushes on my belly. There was silence. The technician leapt to her feet and almost forgot to say she would be back! I pull out my phone and text my favorite person, Christina.

My eyes were shut as I lay relaxed, borderline dozing off. Mrs. Ross, Yes, I replied as the lady and faint figure entered the dark room. There was a bright white light behind them, so I could only make out shadowy figures. A hand touched my leg, soft but concerned. I felt the touch; it was almost angelic. I'm sorry we have lost your little girl. I froze and let out a heart-wrenching scream. It was loud enough that I'm sure everyone in the office felt my pain instantly. Instantly it was as if my body had been lit on fire. I was hot, sweating, confused, and in pain, yet my physical body was unharmed. My heart stopped, and chaos was ensured. There was panic in the room as nurses and technicians rushed about, grabbing medical equipment all to come out to my aid. The background noises all but faded and came to a standstill. I was numb; I was still. Then, in an instant, I came to my senses " I gotta call my husband."

In silence I waited, I heard the nurse ask whether there was someone she could call for me. I was a wreck, sobbing, fumbling, and snorting. My head was pounding. I couldn't remember the number I had just spoken to my husband on just a few moments ago. I finally was able to call Dewayne's phone, no answer. I called and called and called again. I knew he was at work, but I needed to reach him. I mustered the strength to call his work number. I said so few words but said what needed to be said. " Our daughter died." In a second, he was there. He looked disheveled but instantly locked eyes with me, and I broke down again. At that moment, no words were spoken, but our hearts connected. We both lost a little bit of ourselves, right there, in the doctor's office. The gel was still on my belly, now cold, gross, and nauseating.

It seemed like an eternity of crying and sobbing. The nurse with the blood pressure cuff and the small cup of ice-cold water given it to me in hopes that it was supposed to soothe my heart or even my soul. There was a little more commotion; I couldn't fully process what was happening around me. I was like a horse in a race with blinders. I only continued to stare at the black screens and, from time to time, peek open my eyes in hopes this was a nightmare that I would wake up from. Between the tears and the heartache, I also had to take on a new reality, my daughter, Avery. She hadn't moved. She was stillborn.

As the cloud of darkness left the room, the doctor began speaking with me regarding my options. "She's too big to be extracted, and you will need to deliver her. You can choose a c-section or vaginally deliver; that's your choice. " I questioned the word "extracted." I felt she spoke carelessly about my daughter and my options. "Mrs. Ross, we will send your information to the hospital so that there is no paperwork for you. I was silent, still, and numb." Ok", I responded hesitantly." I had no time to think of my options. All of the answers had to be given right then and there. I just answered with one word that would help me get through this ordeal and the next few years of my life. It's time to be strong, exhibit strength, and stop all this crying. It was nothing left for me to do from here. The moments of silence were then filled with, "we will put a pink carnation on the wall for you. It's our sign, so people know not to bother you, but also that your little girl will be born sleeping". That was the first time I heard that term, but I knew what it meant. I wasn't going to cry anymore. I swallowed the ball in my throat that was as tough and scratchy as an SOS pad.

I took that same elevator down in silence while my husband held my hand. There was nothing to be said. Finally, we made it outside, and the sun I enjoyed and welcomed with joy and a warm heart earlier was out with a vengeance. It was hot and beaming only on me, trying to pierce my skin, burning, hot and uncomfortable. I heard the buzzing of bees, which added to my annoyance. Everything outside created anger in me. How did Christina get here? My birth partner, cousin, and best friend came to soothe my soul like a bowl of chicken noodle soup straight from my grandmother's kitchen. I looked up from the ground, and my eyes met hers. I could see it in her demeanor. Her face said it all. She empathized with me, my husband, with my family.

Dewayne opened my door for me, and I plopped in the passenger seat. I left my car, hopes, and happiness in that parking lot to deal with another time. I looked at Dewayne from that passenger seat and said, " I'm not ready to go to the hospital. He just nodded and said ok. I think at that moment, he aged more and more as the seconds passed. It was the first time I noticed the salt and pepper growing aggressively in his beard and the crow's feet creeping in the right by the arm of his glasses. I'm almost certain that those were not there before. I broke his heart. I spoke through the sadness and grief happily as I could. "Let's go to Popeyes; I'm hungry."

As we pull into Popeyes, I see a line that wraps around the building. "Let's go inside. I'm not in a rush," I said this as if we were just on a lunch date and enjoying each other. All three of us, Christina, Dewayne and myself sat down and enjoyed lunch. It was a typical lunch you would expect family members to share if they hadn't just been told their child was dead. But, it was an escape from the impending obstacles in front of me. As we sat and ate, I found humor in my day. ' I guess I'm not going to work today!!" Everyone laughed. And for the next four years, humor was my escape. This moment was family, fellowship, and support that would carry me through every trial and tribulation. These are my people. I looked to my side and out the window as my husband caressed my neck so gently, and a tear dropped. Just one, but it signified I needed to take the next steps. I let everyone know I'm ready to go home. It's time to pack my hospital bag, but just for me.

We pulled into the driveway that normally only held two cars. For some reason, it felt like a never-ending long, winding road. I walked upstairs and past the completely furnished baby-ready nursery. The door was shut, but I could feel the emptiness of the crib and the cold shutter of the missing little person that was supposed to fill that space with joy and laughter. It was a room that would never be filled with my little girl or the cries that needed to be soothed. In that sense, I felt useless. I failed. To the left was my bedroom. The room I had waddled from earlier in the day. We had a small brown leather couch that I would often sit on and put my feet up when I was exhausted from the day's work. The leather couch that once made gave me comfort would now soak up my sorrow and my pains. I sat there for a few eternities before my husband came to check up on me. I was limp. My legs would not allow me to stand to gather the strength to pack the bag of doom—the bag of sadness. I could not push myself to my feet to get the umph to stand and pack. My arms felt as though they had cinder blocks attached. I just laid back.

Time had passed but stood still. I knew this was my last maternity outfit, the last time I would need to jump or wiggle and be exhausted from getting dressed. The door creaked open. Dewayne looked at me and said, "you want me to help?" I laid still but was able to answer. "Sure," in almost a whisper. I told him simply just get me something comfy, no maternity clothes. I wouldn't need them once this was over. My pregnancy would be coming to an end, and I didn't need any reminders.

We left. One bag, no car seat, or cute baby's first outfit to take pictures in. My long braids were pulled up into a beautiful Nubian style bun, wrapped to perfection, yet my eyes still screamed sorrow, red and glassy from the tears that overflowed hours before. I let out a sigh; where tears should have flowed, nothing dropped. I could do this. I could make it to the end. I didn't need to cry. I'm strong, and the lack of tears showed I was the strongest. In the hospital, I walked the winding sterile white hallways with an attitude of fearlessness. The lights were bright, almost blinding, you could hear the distant chatter, but it was still inaudible. I felt all the eyes on me. They all knew why I was there and what I came for. Their faces beamed with fake smiles, but I could see behind them. They felt bad for me, and they felt my pain. They would never wanna feel what I felt, knowing the worse was yet to come. I felt shameful. What was wrong with me? What was I to do to change the outcome of this situation I was entering? Did they think I was on drugs? Did they think I did this on purpose? I was at the receptionist's counter a few doors and sliding doors later.

I walked to the counter, which seemed to be six feet high. The receptionist peered down over the mountain, called a desk, and asked, " Can I get your name?" "Ma'am, your name please"? There by my side, Dewayne was my voice. "Ross, Victoria" He ran down my allergies, medical history, and the regular nonsense that wouldn't change the outcome. I felt like a helpless child. No voice I couldn't advocate for myself or even speak my name? I couldn't show up for myself; just add that to the list of things I've failed at. This woman must think I'm stupid. I know she's calling all her friends and telling them about the most incompetent woman she's ever met. ME!

The sliding doors slammed open and shut. I could hear the buzzing. I could hear the multitude of footsteps. I could hear the doors that separated me from intake to birthing rooms. As we walked, it felt like a professional speed walker was leading us. This lady had things to do, and we were clearly holding her back. She gave her condolences and even insisted she knew what I was going through. While outwardly I was stoic, inside, I was cursing this lady up one side and down the other. I'm sure I called her everything except a child of God.

I saw the carnation. I thought, "This is it, my delivery room." They broke my water, and my labor progressed. I had zero pain. I refused medication, "just ice," I repeated as they questioned my choice of pain management for the contractions that would spike off the monitor. I didn't need mediation because I couldn't feel the pain my body was actually in. I felt aches but nothing out of the norm, maybe a menstrual pain of very low intensity. My heart was too broken actually to feel and be in the moment for the delivery. I closed my eyes and paged the nurse. When she arrived, I asked, "Could you look? I feel something". Two pushes later, she was here. My daughter, my angel, my Avery Christina Ross, was born, I experienced a stillbirth. My mother, who was always too busy to pour into me, too busy to celebrate me, was there to rub my leg and watch as they handled her granddaughter. She was as comforting as she knew, and that was enough for me. I didn't cry, but everyone was there to see my strength. My mommy rubbed my head, and I felt loved for that moment, just that second.

A couple of wipes wrapped in a fresh, crisp receiving blanket. It was the standard issue blue burgundy and white striped receiving blanket all kids received. Before gently laying her on my chest, the doctor spoke lovingly, "here's your angel." I gave half a smirk that barely moved my face. I'm holding my baby for the very first and last time. Avery has been whisked away, weighed, measured, and dressed like a sleeping doll. My doll was still silent, born sleeping, stillborn. I studied her face—the lashes, even her unibrow like her father. I needed to engrain these memories in my brain. I needed to save this memory of my daughter. I never wanted to forget her. This needed to be unforgettable. I held her, my little loaf of bread, and made sure to comfort her. I fixed her little bonnet on her head and made sure she was perfectly wrapped. In my brain, she was already memorialized. I wanted this to be forever. This was for me. This was my last memory of her because she would never grow up. This was going to be as perfect as the first day of school picture I would never get.

When we left the hospital, I wasn't ready. I looked for every reason why I needed to stay and why I needed to be there. In my heart, I knew that I would be leaving my Avery. No funeral ensued, not even a small memorial. I wish my grandmother could have led a small prayer for her. I left my daughter in the hospital, not knowing what would happen to her body. I just knew I opted for the autopsy that would give me the answers I could not answer myself. All parts of me felt defeated, useless, and empty. I decided to return to work two weeks later. That proved I was strong. I threw myself into every committee and excelled. I flourished in all things that were a distraction to what was really going on in my life.

Five months later, I was pregnant again with a boy. I was diagnosed with gestational diabetes, every prenatal condition most women dread, and preeclampsia plagued my pregnancy, but I was able to deliver that bouncing boy without a hitch. No signs of postpartum, no significant weight gain, and I was stunning from start to finish. He was another easy labor and delivery. I knew I had an issue when I cried at my ultrasound and found out it was a girl. That's right, my son was now eight months old, and we were pregnant again. Again, I sobbed tears of sadness or fear, knowing what the last pregnancy with a girl resulted in. Every day I did my kick counts, my prenatal vitamins, and everything I could to make sure this didn't end the same my pregnancy with Avery did. While we never truly got answers after going through the autopsy and nonstop bloodwork for both her and myself. I wanted this pregnancy to turn out differently, but I couldn't even gather myself to share the excitement.

In the day and age of social media, I didn't post photos of myself or my growing belly. Nobody knew anything. I didn't speak a word about this pregnancy. I did not prep or plan an elaborate baby shower or even an announcement. This was all too much to handle. Every day I woke up in fear. I feared that this would be the last day of pregnancy, ending in death. Finally, around 32 weeks of pregnancy, Christina calls me and fusses with me as usual. Usually in pregnancy she would tell me to leave her alone and let her do her planning, this was not my norm. When Vicky is not in control normally i'm out of control. This time during her call she was practically pleading with me just to tell people I was pregnant because they had begun plans for a baby shower. I was completely hands-off and not even slightly joyous.

The Facebook post went like this:

"Hey, I'm pregnant; it's a girl. Baby shower invitations will be sent out shortly." That was my grand announcement. I didn't want to discuss it, so any calls I received, or texts were ignored. I didn't want to explain another loss to a mass audience.

Once again, it was delivery day, but there was a problem, I did not pick a name. What was I going to name this girl, baby? Oh well didn't matter to me. It would be another name on a death certificate that would cause me more pain. My husband did the naming. Taylor Victoria, after two people that mean the most to him. Lawrence Taylor, from the New York Giants, and his amazing black queen. Taylor came bouncing into this world earlier than expected. She went to the NICU before I could hold her. Well, I guess now it's only a matter of time before I hear some devastating news. I could not see her because they gave me medication that would make me a fall risk. I was confined to a bed, a room alone. Dewayne went to visit her for the first 24 hours, only sharing pictures. I didn't know this child and couldn't even bond with her. The issues and fears of a stillborn reared their ugly head. Issues that now had gone unnoticed, unresolved, were here in my face in the forefront. Ten days later, and after a NICU stay, I was home with this baby I couldn't bond with.

I knew my issues were not normal, but I didn't know where to turn. Postpartum had set in, and I was lost. My house was a mess, and nobody noticed. I know my housekeeping was talked about, my hair standing on top of my head, and probably the last time I showered was probably a topic of conversation. I could not shake these feelings, the fear, the catastrophic thinking that she would die each time she took a nap. Or even if I slept longer than an hour, she would cry until she couldn't breathe and choke on her spit. I couldn't shake this fear. I couldn't get myself into a routine. I couldn't enjoy having a girl child. I could not mother a child I continually feared I would lose.

I sought help. I asked around for recommendations. I desperately needed to be fixed in my first few sessions. I knew we connected. She looked like me. She was a mother. She was married and understood my lingo. Those sessions were intense. I remember taking my sessions on my iPad in my closet. Week after week, she would say, "are we still in the closet" while we joked about it; I felt it was her way of asking if I was still holding onto my pain. Eventually, we progressed, and I came out of the closet for most sessions. I cried less and smiled more. I went out one day without my kids, and nobody died. I began to live my life the way it was meant to be. I am no longer in fear that if anything happened, it would be the end of someone's life, my daughter's life. I went to Avery's memorial site and spent time and read to her, even making sure she got a Gift on her birthday. I was a bereaved mother but still had some fight in me to heal.

As I've journeyed through years of continued grief and self-loathing, some of me hated myself. I no longer wanted to carry those burdens. At the same time, it pains me to have never gotten concrete answers on what caused my daughter's demise. I'm ready to let go of my trauma. As a mother of three living children, I know I'm a protector and have no reason to blame myself. Because I couldn't get medically sound answers, it was easier to blame myself simply because I found fault in changing the day. I went to my doctor's appointment. When speaking about my daughter, I no longer carry shame and guilt but a calling to be an educator and an advocate for legislation. I do this to alleviate the burdens and financial stress of non-medically necessary testing, second and third opinions, and even autopsies that are not covered by health insurance. $4189.14 is the bill that greeted me when my arms, my daughter's crib, and my heart was empty. While my daughter is not here physically, she's given me a push to be open and speak about the loss of a child. That gave me the strength to carry on and the ability to leave behind shame and guilt.

My healing and growth have not been linear in any sense. I still cry, grieve, and even suffer anxiety with depressive episodes when my daughter simply gets a cough or chokes on something she shouldn't have. I will always fear for her life. I'm showing that anxiety may be able to rear its head from time to time, but because I'm here and can vocalize my pain, it has not won. Despite my storm, I am a survivor.

LETTER TO SELF

Vicky,

Life will throw you curve balls and you will face many trials and tribulations. Therapy will help you navigate emotions and figure out what you want and how to handle all things including the loss of the most precious being to be created, your daughter. Learn not to blame yourself and let others help you. You don't always have to struggle alone and block others out. It's smart to protect your heart but are you really just blocking a blessing? Ask questions, stand up for yourself, and be bold in who you are. In due time you will find yourself, your happiness, and even your life partner. Have fun, live life, travel and continue to take what life gives you knowing you're undefeated and your thirties will be good to you.

Enjoy,
Thirty-four year old Mrs. Victoria Ross

CHAPTER FOURTEEN

Its All In Your Head

Shelley Puchalsky

HIVES

As I sat in the blue plastic chair with the rigid back and four metal legs attached at each corner of the cold hard plastic, I heard the school nurse's voice in the distance on the phone. She was talking to my mom. I could barely make out what she was saying, but every now and then, I would catch a few words here and there in between the glimpses she would shoot towards me. "Mrs. Reali? Yes. I'm not sure. You'll have to come and get her. They're red, raised bumps. She'll need to see the doctor."

My mom came into the nurse's office hurriedly with big poofy brown hair like she had just stepped out of a Farrah Fawcett commercial. She had big brown eyes, dangly gold earrings, a white lace bodysuit with poofy sleeves tucked into her acid-washed jeans, topped off with her scrunchy 2-inch brown leather boots.

She scooped me up and carried me to the car. At this point, the hives had covered my entire body, including my feet, and I could not put shoes on. She drove me straight to the doctor's office on the military base. I could hear her pleading with the receptionist to please allow us to come back and see the doctor. The receptionist told her they were busy, and I could not be seen. My mom started crying. "Look at her; just look at my baby; someone, please help my baby!" Finally, the receptionist looked over at me and said, "Let me see what I can do."

They gave me some Prednisone and Atarax to help clear the reaction. They had no idea what started the reaction. I've spent most of my life wondering what caused that horrible episode. And I've spent most of my life dealing with similar unresolved episodic health issues. What I didn't know was how significant of an impact these unresolved issues would have on me 30 years after a minor laceration to my face.

MIGRAINES

From around the age of seven, I would lay in my parent's bed writhing in pain from migraines. First, they would come on full force like a steaming freight train was running through the middle of my forehead. They would appear out of nowhere, seemingly unprovoked, and leave me totally incapacitated. I remember laying there on the bed, crying with a cold washcloth over my head. These migraines continued well into my mid-20s.

I would go to the ER for these migraines, and it was always the same routine. They would give me a shot of Toradol and tell me to follow up with the neurologist. After that, there was never much else that they would do for me.

STOMACH PAINS

I had always been picked on for having a rather sensitive stomach and sense of smell. As a teenager, I remember I wanted to fit in and simply try sausage even though the smell of it bothered me. So, I took a few bites of the rubbery meat. I woke up around 2:00 AM with the most violent stomach pain ever. I began vomiting with an intensity that I had never experienced before. The vomiting woke my mother up. I ended up throwing up all night into the following day when my mother finally took me into the emergency room. Since we lived in Germany, things were a little different over there. I was mortally embarrassed when I was told I had to disrobe and take everything off, including bras and underwear, to get weighed. I was so sick I ended up vomiting and defecating myself at the same time, which I was incredibly embarrassed by being that I was a teenager and overall, just feeling very weak and not knowing what happened to me. I genuinely thought it had been the meat with the rubbery texture I had eaten. When they ran some tests, they discovered it was not food poisoning. They told me that the problem was my appendix. They had set me on the schedule to have surgery in the morning. They came in my room promptly at 8:00 AM and put me on a cold metal table, and as I was staring up at the ceiling, ready for them to come in to put me to sleep, the doctor came in and put his hand on my shoulder and said it turns out we do not need to do the surgery after all because the last test on your appendix came back fine. Yet again, another strange episodic event with no warning or explanation behind why my appendix was inflamed and I was just sent home.

FAINTING SPELLS

When I was about 19 years old, reality TV was big; since I lived with my cousin, we would enjoy binge sessions together. I remember sitting there this one day, and I started to get a strange aura as if maybe I needed to get up and get some food in the kitchen. It felt like my mouth was beginning to water like I was having trouble swallowing. So, I stood up. I went to walk into the kitchen to make myself some carrots with peanut butter. I remember my cousin speaking to me, and everything seemed to move slowly. I was chuckling at whatever she was saying but couldn't really respond. I had no sooner put the carrots in the bowl with the peanut butter and turned to walk back into the living room when I passed out in the hallway doorway. It was as if the sand through an hourglass was pouring through my mind, and everything faded into black. It was very slow and super subtle. My aunt's boyfriend started yelling "Shelley, Shelley, are you okay?" He then picked me up and carried me over onto the couch. I was sweating and felt cold and clammy. I couldn't respond, and I was confused. I wanted to brush it off like it hadn't happened because I didn't have an explanation for what just happened. I thought to myself, maybe I hadn't eaten enough that day, or maybe it was just my sugar. I didn't tell anyone what had happened because I didn't think it was a big deal until it happened about a month later again. This time I was at a friend's house. When we were all sitting around watching television, there were about six of us. My best friend Ashley was there. I started to get a strange aura again, the same strange feeling I had before. I stood up and thought let me find some peanut butter. I got up to walk into the kitchen and find some peanut butter, but I wasn't fast enough. Whatever it had been just hit me like a ton of bricks. Again, just the feeling of sand through an hourglass. Darkness came over me.

Everything turned pitch black. But this time, there was shaking that I couldn't control. I could hear my best friend running towards me. I could hear her cries "Shelley, Shelley, are you okay?" I could hear my friend Josh "Shelley! Are you okay?" I could hear Ashley yell "Her eyes are rolling into the back of her head; call 911!" I could hear everything they were saying, but I couldn't move and couldn't talk. But apparently, I was shaking on the outside, and my eyes were rolling in the back of my head. I wanted to speak and say I was okay. I wanted to say, "I can hear you, I'm okay!" But I couldn't say anything. I remember the ambulance taking me and putting me on the stretcher. I felt so embarrassed, and I don't know why. I didn't want to go to the hospital. I didn't want to find out if there was anything wrong with me. I just wanted to be normal. I was scared that this episode was just another example of a medical mystery that I might have or may be.

NUMBNESS/TINGLING

I remember shortly after being put on birth control, I started to have trouble with numbness and tingling in my arm and in my right leg. I remember going into the emergency room. I always hate the smell of those rooms. There's a coldness in the air, and something about the smell makes your stomach turn. They could never answer why I was experiencing what I was experiencing, and I always left feeling so helpless. They told me it was more than likely just anxiety, which oddly enough I didn't feel a sense of anxiety until after I left the hospital with no diagnosis, questioning my own reality of my symptoms. I suddenly felt uneasy about the symptoms I had been experiencing, and I began to learn to not acknowledge or trust my own body and my own brain. I began to question every symptom that I would have to a point that I would let things go for months and months until they were a symptom that could no longer be avoided.

ENDOMETRIOSIS

After the birth of my first son, I begin having incredible pain in my pelvic area. At first, the doctors told me that it was psychological because I had just had a baby. I kept telling them I felt like it was something physical. It felt like there was something right there bulging out of that area. Instead, they gave me Valium and told me that I just needed to connect with my husband more. I went to another doctor, who performed some tests and said I had endometriosis. When she went in with the scope, she told me that my uterus was fused to my ovaries with scar tissue. I saw another doctor after that, who diagnosed me with pelvic organ prolapse. That wasn't until after the birth of my second son, which means I had been walking around with prolapsing internal organs for almost two years.

MORE FAINTING SPELLS

It was a hot summer day, my son Jackson was about a year and a half, and I was about six months pregnant with my son Roman. I was at a checkup appointment for Jackson. This episode came on like nothing. I was standing there talking one minute, and the next minute everything started moving in slow motion, and I knew what was coming. I couldn't breathe. My vision started to go. I hit the ground like a ton of bricks. I was so scared. I thought I was going to die in front of my baby. Thankfully it happened at a doctor's office, so they could hold Jackson and take care of him while my husband came to get him and took me to the hospital. They checked on the baby, and he was fine. They didn't know what had happened to me.

TROUBLE BREATHING

Immediately after the birth of my son Roman, I started getting a metallic taste in my mouth and I couldn't breathe. I called out to the nurse and let her know my symptoms as they were increasing severely. I saw the look of sheer terror in my husband's eyes. They put me on oxygen, and I started to feel better. But they had no explanation for what had happened to me. So just as always, I stuffed down the experience and the sad feelings associated with it and pretended that it never happened to me.

SURGERY

To fix my pelvic organ prolapse, I needed to have surgery. I had never had surgery before and was a little nervous. However, I seemed to be doing fine after the surgery. Ten days later, I was cleared to fly to Las Vegas with my (now) ex-husband because he was the best man at a wedding. I remember before boarding the plane I was having a little bit of pulling pain on the left side of my pelvic area. I still had some bleeding which I thought might be a little unusual, but the doctor assured me it was fine.

So shortly after we arrived, I told my husband I was going to lie down. I remember feeling like I was peeing myself, so I pulled the covers back. I couldn't believe what I was seeing. There was blood just pouring out of me. Like someone was taking a two-liter bottle and squirting blood from between my legs. I was hemorrhaging. I had to go by ambulance to the hospital and have emergency surgery to fix the internal bleeding. It was a blood clot on a major artery in my pelvic area. They aren't sure why it happened.

You would think that would be the end of that, but it wasn't. Shortly afterward, I told my doctor I didn't think the incision was healing correctly. They assured me it was fine. At this point, a giant purple lump was on the left side of the incision, about the size of a baseball. I had to go back about three times to get them to listen to me, and finally, one of the other doctors in the office told me I had a hematoma that needed to be popped and drained. I was left with an open wound for six months.

DISFIGUREMENT

The events leading up to my disfigurement are sometimes difficult for me to capture into words. I go back to those moments leading up to everything that happened and all the doctor's appointments, and I try to make sense of it all, but I'm not sure I ever will. I was out for a run with my dog when she stopped abruptly in front of me, causing me to fall and land on my face. I had two lacerations, one on my forehead and one on my nose. I ended up getting stitches, and the stitches became infected. I went to a plastic surgeon. He assured me he could help. He did a skin graft where he took skin from behind my ear and put it on my nose. After that, he stitched my forehead closed.

I noticed right away that my left eyebrow was much higher than my right eyebrow, and there was a lot of redness in both areas. When I told him that my eyebrow was a lot higher and I was having difficulty moving it, he said "You came to me with a hole in your forehead, and I fixed it; what else do you want from me?" He seemed highly annoyed. I also noticed that a red line started to appear, traveling up a vein from where the stitches were on my forehead up into my scalp. When I called the doctor's office, they told me they didn't have any appointments for a few weeks but that if it were terrible, I could go into the emergency room. So, I went into the emergency room. The attending physician said it looked to him as if I had an infection and they were going to go ahead and admit me but that he needed to call my surgeon. He came back into the room a few minutes later with a look of shock and told me my surgeon said I was okay and to send me home.

I felt like I'd been punched in the gut. What transpired from there was months upon months of me going from doctor to doctor. I was so sick that I could barely stand up at times. I had a 4 1/2 hemoglobin— and was therefore sent to a hematologist who then ordered a slew of tests including a bone marrow biopsy because the doctors were convinced that I had cancer. I had to do iron infusions. I had to do an MRI, which is where they discovered that I had an infection in the bone in my skull called osteomyelitis. None of the doctors I were seeing told me that I needed to see an infectious disease doctor during this time. I figured that out on my own. By the time I made it to an infectious disease doctor, it was the day before Thanksgiving.

So, it had been a little over a year since my original injury, and I had undergone two surgeries. It turns out that I was septic from the osteomyelitis infection in the bone in my skull, meaning it had traveled through my blood system.

I'll never know how close I was to dying, but I feel it was relatively close. The scarring I've been left with on my face and scalp is difficult to look at and bring up in a conversation. I can't help but feel so angry and mistreated because the scarring that I have been left with would not have been as bad as it is had the doctors helped me a year prior. My third surgery consisted of an incision made from ear to ear, a drain placed in my scalp which left a large bald spot, a bald spot above my right ear, a small bald spot on the top of my scalp, and an incision down the side of my face from the top of my nose all the way down the smile line and a little further. It makes me sad to mourn the loss of my old face when I think about how easily it could have been for them to put me on an IV PICC line of antibiotics as they did one year later.

I'm facing multiple corrective surgeries. I have trouble opening my mouth fully because of the scarring on the right side of my cheek. I will never have movement of the upper left side of my face. Every day when I look in the mirror, it's a constant reminder of how the medical system has failed me. It's a constant reminder of me as a tiny six-year-old girl coming into them with hives, migraines, fainting spells, stomach pain, and being told there's nothing wrong with you; it's all in your head. Except for this time, it really was in my head. An actual infection was inside my head, and they let me suffer for a year.

The doctors let me suffer at my own expense, at the cost of my face… a face that is no longer familiar to me. A face that I struggle to look at every day in the mirror. A face that I no longer recognize anymore. A face that I must relearn every wrinkle, every curve, every flaw, every imperfection. A face that I have learned to mask so that it doesn't look scary or bad to the outside world. A face that I love to cover up with masks (thanks Covid!), makeup, hats, and glasses. I've learned that there's more to life than just how my face looks. But at the same time, that is always the first thing people see when they meet you. That's been the most challenging part of my journey. I am figuring out how to adjust to people's thoughts when they first see my face. Do I tell them what happened? Do I pretend like it's not noticeable? I'm still on my journey, so I don't have the answers to these questions. With that said, I continue telling myself I'm strong, worthy, and a warrior, and I have the scars to prove it, internally and externally.

ANTIPHOSPHOLIPID ANTIBODY SYNDROME

I recently was diagnosed with an autoimmune disorder called antiphospholipid antibody syndrome (APS). This is my second autoimmune disorder diagnosis, my first is hyperthyroidism, which means my thyroid functions too fast at times. APS is a disorder where the immune system mistakenly attacks normal proteins in the blood. This means I am at an increased risk for blood clots to form in the arteries, veins, and organs. It can cause miscarriage (which I have experienced) and fatigue (which I absolutely have experienced). In a way, I am grateful that my journey has led me to a place where this diagnosis was made possible. But of course, there is this part of me that wishes that I didn't have an autoimmune disorder because I just want to be like everyone else. I'm not sure that this autoimmune disorder explains all the things that have happened to me, but it gave me a lot of insight into some of the medical mysteries that I have experienced. I'm proud of myself for not giving up this entire time and pushing through all the doctor's appointments and all the let downs, because it finally got me a diagnosis.

I'm not fully sure that my diagnosis ends at APS, as I sometimes wonder if I have something else in conjunction with the APS. I sometimes wonder if I have Lupus like my mother does. I watched her suffer from about the age of 8 to 24 when she was finally diagnosed, and I know that autoimmune can be difficult to diagnose. The average patient spends about ten years before they're properly diagnosed with autoimmune diseases, so I know it's not an easy or quick road. I'm just glad that I have the grit to keep fighting for the answers and the mental strength to always keep fighting no matter what comes my way.

LETTER TO SELF

Dear Shelley,

I know that what you're going through is tough. You have no control over your own body. The hives. The migraines. You're so young. You are confused. You feel like you can't trust yourself. Or your own body. Or any of the adults around you. Nobody can help you or understand you.

But you can help yourself. Listen to yourself. Listen to your body. The welts won't last forever. The migraines won't last forever. The pain in your belly won't last forever. I know it seems invisible to others, but you're not the only person with this pain. It's not anything you did.

You'll have to fight harder and be stronger than other little girls. You're going to get jealous of how carefree their lives are. That's okay. What's meant for you isn't meant for them. I promise what's waiting at the end for you is far greater and richer than what you have ever imagined.

Maybe you're looking at your current situation and you're going to feel like giving up, but I promise you that will not happen.

You're going to face a lot of adversity, and you're going to have to fight HARD. Keep going. Don't ever stop. You're not wrong about what you feel inside your body.

You are strong, brave, and worthy of love.

With love,
Shelley

CHAPTER FIFTEEN

That House

Zionne Malloy

I used to live at my mom's house. I got to my dad's house by telling lies on my mom. My stepmom made me lie in court to make my mom look bad. If I didn't lie, I would get yelled at and shamed by my dad's side. I was young, so I didn't want to get yelled at, so I did what I was told. I felt a little bad lying, but my mom and I's relationship wasn't the best. She was dealing with the divorce and now being a single mom, so if I did something wrong, like not doing my chores, she would be angrier than she would be because of the pent-up stress. She would take a little bit of anger out on me. Afterward, she would apologize, but I was too focused on her doing it in the first place to forgive her. Before court dates, my stepmom would plan a script for me to follow. It was painful telling those lies to my mom. After all the plotting and scheming, I moved to my dad's house.

My dad's house was not great. The house was almost 100 years old, and I was close enough to walk to the school. The house was always filthy. We had five dogs and three cats that I had to look after even though all I had was a cat that always ran away. Everyone was too lazy to clean up the house but me. The house was so old that it was falling apart, the tiles were coming off, and one time I was going up the stairs, and the stair fell. The house always smelled, and there were fleas everywhere. There were mice in the ceiling, in the walls, and on the couch. There was no gas in the house or running water for some time. There was never hot water in the house, so sometimes we went to the gym to shower.

Living in the house was super tedious. Doing simple actions like taking a shower was a whole process. First, I had to get this big pot and fill it with water. Then, I had to put it on the stove and wait for it to get hot. After it got hot, I took it to the bathroom and cooled it with some cold water. Then, I had to use a cup to pour water on myself from the pot. I had to cook things on an electric food warmer when there was no gas.

At first, I just endured it, hoping it would improve, but it never did. I hated eating, taking a shower, and doing things everyone else did. All I ever wanted to do was to get out of that house. I spent most of my time sleeping. If I was asleep, I wasn't hungry; if I wasn't hungry, I didn't have to eat. If I didn't have to eat, then I didn't have to go into the kitchen to make something to eat. When I was awake, I watched anime because I was so focused on reading the subtitles and comprehending the story that I didn't notice everything else that was happening in the house.

Being in that house washed me away as a person. My memory got worse, and I didn't have a personality. The things I liked were taken away because they didn't understand and said they were evil. I still struggle with "all about me worksheets that we have to do in school. My sister and I were treated differently. She was pampered and spoiled. Every time my dad or my stepmom told me to clean our rooms. My sister would call her grandmother and tell her to clean her room. When her grandmother came to clean her room, she brought a bunch of snacks. Then when I asked for her help, I was called lazy and told to do it myself. When I wanted a 50-cent bag of chips, I was told to go make some money and buy it myself. When my sister left to go to her friend's house, I was left at the house by myself and was forced to do her chores when she wasn't there. If I left to go help out my grandmother, nobody did my chores, and I was yelled at for not doing them. I had to do whatever my sister wanted to do, or she would tell our parents, and I would be yelled at for being mean to her. My existence there was second class.

On Tuesday, November 10, 2020, during the Covid-19 pandemic, I stayed home from hybrid school. The medication that I was on caused me to throw up. I emailed my teachers on Schoology (I was in 6th grade). I told them that I wasn't going to be on zoom or in class because I was sick. Around 7:30 a.m. I went downstairs to go find some food that didn't have to be microwaved. On my way to the kitchen, my stepmom stopped me in my tracks. She told me to clean up the house, take out the dogs and feed the ones outside even though my sister was the one who was supposed to feed them. I painstakingly did those chores and cleaned up the house. As I was cleaning, my stepmom and my dad went somewhere. My stepsister and I were home alone like always.

After I had spent 3 hours doing those chores, I went to sleep. I woke up around 5 when I heard my dad pull into the driveway. I went downstairs, and my dad gave my stepsister 15 dollars. "What was that for?" I asked. My dad said it was my sister who cleaned up the house. We got paid for doing it. I told him that it was me who cleaned up the house and that my sister was upstairs all day except to get food. My stepmom yelled and said, "Are you calling my baby a lair?" I blatantly said yes, and she told me to get out of her face.

The next day was veterans' day. I didn't know it was Veterans Day. I thought it was on Thursday. There was no school, and I just spent the day watching Anime. I went downstairs and went to my dad in the kitchen. I told him that he should stop spending money on my stepmom because she was cheating on him. I also told him that I saw the proof on her phone. My stepmom came stomping through the kitchen and said, "He already knows I'm cheating on him, so there's no point in telling him." I left the room just flabbergasted. As I was leaving, I called my stepmom a stupid idiot in Japanese. My dad asked me what it meant, and when I told him, he was pretty upset. A couple of minutes later, my sister's grandmother called me on google duo. She was yelling and screaming at me because I said that my stepmom was cheating even though she said it herself. She said, " I'm glad my mom punched you in the face, even though it did not happen, and I can't wait for you to get out of that house. I said I would get rid of myself and decided to run away. I was caught and had to talk to these crisis hotline people. After that, I went to sleep.

The next day I can't remember if there was school or not. I thought it was veterans' day. I made a veterans day post on Facebook, and my sister's grandmother took it the wrong way. She started saying horrible things to me again, which I wasn't going to take. I argued back and forth with her for a while, but my dad came upstairs to take my phone. He took it, and I was locked upstairs in my room because I said I was going to leave.

I was trying to go to sleep around five because tomorrow I was going with my mom, and I wanted to get through the rest of the day sleeping. My sister came into my room telling me we were going bowling. I was skeptical. Why would they take me bowling? I brushed it off, thinking they would make me watch or just get on good terms. My dad took me to Dunkin Donuts, and I got a ghost pepper donut. We returned to the house to pick up my sister and stepmom. We drove for a while and were at "the bowling alley." It was a mental hospital. As we were walking in there, my dad held me down, which I didn't understand until we got there. Until we got in, I thought it was a bowling alley. My dad told me what was happening, and I burst into tears. I wanted to see my brother the next day. So, when they interviewed me, I tried to sound like I was perfectly fine. In the end, my efforts were futile after my dad insisted on me staying there. I was an inpatient there for a week, which was fun. I didn't know why I was there, but the people were nice. The people asked me what I wanted to get out of staying there, and I said to go back with my mom. After one week, they made it happen; by the time I got out, it was Thanksgiving break.

The mental hospital was not as bad as I thought it would be. It was better than being at my dad's house. I had running water and food that didn't have to be microwaved. I didn't have to be worried about doing my sister's chores or doing things that

I didn't want to do with my sister. When I wanted to take a shower, I didn't have to use a pot of water. I could just use the shower. If I didn't want to talk to the other people there, I didn't have to. Being there was great, apart from not being able to watch anime or play the Xbox.

After I got out, my mom took me shopping for new clothes, shoes, and other things that I didn't have at the house. Soon after we got home, the police with my stepmom came to get the clothes off my back. Little did she know, we had already dropped those clothes off at their house. We knew that she would come back for the clothes. After all that had happened, it was weird for everything to adjust. I had to sleep in my brother's room because there was mold in my room in the basement. It was a little weird for mom to have to me back in the house because of everything that had happened. I did miss not having my cat around. I don't feel sad about what happened anymore because I passed it, and now I'm having a good time with my mom and little brother, who is taller than me.

My relationship with my mom is better now. She's not as angry, and I don't do things I'm not supposed to. Sometimes I might forget or mess up, but my mom understands. We watch shows and talk about stuff daily. We have a way better relationship where we have fun, and there's understanding on both sides.

LETTER TO SELF

Dear Little Me,

Things may be hard now but keep going. It does get better. Eat healthier and exercise more. The rambling of our father is coming to fruition. Make sure you try your hardest to get Maine because our mom will let him in the house. Practice more on learning Japanese, which will help you later. Try not to let those grades slip. We need straight A's for a scholarship. That's all from me later, buster. There is no sus in supposed.

Made in the USA
Middletown, DE
24 November 2022

15637007R00149